Becoming a
Peaceful Mom

Becoming a
Peaceful Mom

Through Every Season of Raising Your Child

Teresa deBorde Glenn

RESOURCE *Publications* · Eugene, Oregon

Resource Publications
An Imprint of Wipf and Stock Publishers
199 W. 8th Ave., Suite 3
Eugene, OR 97401

www.wipfandstock.com

PAPERBACK ISBN: 978-1-4982-9327-3
HARDCOVER ISBN: 978-1-4982-9329-7
EBOOK ISBN: 978-1-4982-9328-0

Manufactured in the U.S.A.   09/27/16

In honor of Mom and Dad, who poured their best into me

***

To Terrell, the love of my life,
and
to Terrell, Ellison and Carter, and Cecilia—my joy and delight

Contents

Acknowledgements

My heart is in these pages. Much of my sharing results from lots of trial and error and prayer. My stories are samples of treasured markers for where God worked powerfully in me. I pray that your stories become the same for you.

Terrell, I am still amazed that God gave me you. You have loved me, listened, encouraged, supported, inspired, and prayed from the first day I mentioned this book idea. Thank you. I cherish every year of raising our children together. You are a great dad. I love you.

Terrell, Ellison, and Cecilia, you make my heart full. The most rewarding experience of my life is being your mom and watching you grow. God has used you greatly to help me understand grace and how much he loves me. I treasure every season we lived life together. I love you.

To all of you who have prayed for me through this journey: Many times I had to shelve this work, and you encouraged and prayed for me through it all. My heart is full with thanks for you.

To all the moms who have attended my classes and read my blog: Your heartfelt sharing and encouragement lift me up more than you know.

To my author friends: Thank you for your encouragement, for answering my many questions, and for truly being sisters in this journey of writing.

To Alysia Yates: Thank you for your helpful edits and structural insights.

~ My favorite people ~

Teresa and her husband Terrell live in Houston, Texas. Connect with Teresa at celebratethefamily.org.

PART ONE

Define Your Ordinary

1

We Need Answers

IF I JUST HAD a few minutes of peace! Why is it so evasive? Maybe I don't really understand what peace is . . .

At my wit's end, I reached for an old children's dictionary on the bookcase. *An elementary definition is all my frazzled mind can absorb.* One definition described peace as quiet or calm. I laughed out loud when I read the sentence example: "He lived alone in the mountains and enjoyed *peace* of mind." *If I lived alone in the mountains, I would probably have peace of mind too!*

Some days run smoothly, but others feel so chaotic. Who doesn't daydream about having a few hours alone? I want to experience being peaceful—at home with my kids. There has to be a way.

Illusions of a quick fix seduce us: I'll be a different person when . . . Things will settle down around here when . . . Life would be simpler if . . . We are convinced that a change (or two) within our circumstances—employing a cleaning service, finishing a home project, finding a less demanding job, or placing our children in a few more programs—is the key to a more calm and self-controlled *me.* Unfortunately, changes like these only temporarily convey the peace we crave.

How do we become and remain a peaceful mom? In the midst of the noisy chatter and unpredictable moments that each day surely brings, we can experience peace daily, and it won't cost us a dime. The source of this anchoring peace is God.

SAY GOODBYE

"What was I thinking? Don't get me wrong; I love being a mom . . . but I had no idea it would be this hard." My friend, a mother of four, unloaded feelings common to many moms. Being a mom is amazing—and amazingly hard. An entirely new, ever-evolving dimension to how we see and know ourself is triggered.

Some of us dreamed about being a mom and having several kids. Now we have them, and it's not at all what we had imagined! Reality has set in: Being the mom is not like babysitting or being the fun aunt. We keep the children all the time—there is no hand-off! We feel unprepared and sometimes paralyzed with self-doubt.

Homebound or schedule-bound due to our child's needs, we try to adjust to the loss of personal freedom:

- Going to the store: It takes twice as long to pull everything and everyone together, just to get out the door.

- At the store: Shopping is a team event and a fuller experience. Now it includes teaching, pacifying, maybe correcting, and finding roaming children.

- If we are employed: Our personal time before and after work has become a time to process and plan family-oriented matters.

- Meeting a friend for lunch or going out with our husband: It takes twice as long to find an open date and costs twice as much to go—that is, if we find a babysitter.

- If we have left a career or job we enjoyed: We miss the relationships, the intellectual stimulation, and perhaps an aspect of personal identity.

Whatever our adjustment is, life as we knew it has changed. Unfortunately, many of us don't process this fact. We add on this big change, try to resume a prior rhythm, and move forward, sort of. Big change is worth marking to identify what is different, how we feel about it, and how to wisely move forward.

My husband and I were thrilled to learn I was pregnant. After much discussion and prayer, we agreed I would leave my career and stay home once the baby came. As much as I enjoyed being a stay-at-home mom, I missed teaching. I did not realize how daily tangible rewards like interaction with faculty, a clearly defined purpose, and evidence of fruit from my efforts impacted me. My mood swung up as I delighted in my baby boy and swung down when I missed the classroom and all that it represented.

Tired of weekly highs and lows, I realized it was time to mark a season's end—to say good-bye to a former lifestyle. I marked my big change through a prayer. First, I thanked God for all the years and memories I cherished as a teacher. Next, I identified what I missed about it and released these things and that season to him to mark its end. To mark my new beginning, I thanked God for the opportunity to be a mom and to stay at home. I asked him to fill the voids created from leaving my job and to teach me how to live into this big change. For the next three years, as each new school year began, I felt a pull on my heart to return to the classroom. When I gave my feelings to God, the pull lessened. Peace and clarity of purpose for being home increased.

Practice: Mark Change

1. Thank God for the season that is ending.
2. Identify what you will miss.
3. Release these things and release the season to God.
4. Thank God for the new opportunity he is presenting.
5. Ask God to fill all voids if/when you feel them.
6. Invite God to lead you forward.

Ironically, ten years later, I returned to full-time employment. I took time to recognize that my season as a stay-at-home mom had ended. With a mixture of sadness, gratitude, and anticipation for what this big change might be like, I released that season to God. At times, we will realize that life has changed. The sooner we let go or say good-bye to the way life was and welcome God's design for raising our children, the sooner we can embrace and enjoy our new season as women who are *moms*.

DISCOVERY OVERLOAD

From day one as a mom and as our family grows, new dimensions of our character unfold. We identify strengths and weaknesses. We discover qualities in our personality that we never knew were there. For instance, we're more animated than we imagined or not as patient as we assumed.

At the same time, our child learns about himself, experiencing many firsts in an ever-changing environment as he grows up. From the time he's a baby, he trusts us, as he opens his mouth to have all kinds of flavors and textures put in. He discovers the parts of his body and what they do. He tries to learn to make his mouth form words and assumes that we can understand him. As he enters various environments, he adjusts to verbal boundaries like "Yes, you can" or "No, don't touch that," and he learns to interpret our facial expressions and voice tones. He continues to meet people in our extended family, neighborhood, church, school, and the surrounding community. And as he meets peers, he observes them, their behavior, and their parental relationships.

As we take our child places, introduce him to more people, and mingle with other parents, we realize we need to devise and periodically evaluate defined expectations for our child—rules, manners, and anything else we think he needs to learn. Then we have to figure out how we are going to teach these things. As the child receives our instruction, he decides what to do with what he is taught. Sometimes he listens; sometimes he doesn't. Sometimes he obeys; sometimes he doesn't. This relational process continues through his teen years.

Are you tired yet?!

If you're overwhelmed by the current season with your child or feel the burden of the complexities ahead, you are not alone. Feeling inadequate is a familiar trait among the sisterhood of mothers.

"He who calls you is faithful; he will surely do it" (1 Thessalonians 5:24). This is good news. God has purposes that he wants to accomplish through us. He is with us, for us, and *he will do it.*

SEE OUR NEED

Our parenting efforts evolve from a conglomeration of the methods of our parents, our friends, what we read, hear, and observe, and our own ideas. Perhaps we pray for our kids or ourselves regularly. More often desperation or discouragement catalyzes prayer from the reverberating pain in our heart.

Many of us unintentionally compartmentalize our relationship with God. He wants our relationship with him to permeate every aspect of how we live. Specifically as mothers, he wants us to partner with him as we raise our children.

When I am overwhelmed or disheartened, I claim what I know is true: Our Creator *knows* my capabilities, and with all-knowing confidence he gave me the responsibility of being a mother. This rekindles my conviction to live into God's confidence in me, rather than trying to muster self-confidence. On occasion, wearily yet resolutely I pray aloud in my house: *God, you believe in me. You believe I can do this, with your help. Help me trust you.*

Consider this scenario: Knowing my five-year-old daughter's capabilities, I call her to swim across the pool to me. She is anxious, hesitant, lacks self-confidence, yet she trusts me. By experience, she knows that I love her and only challenge her when I believe she can succeed. Because of her trust in me, she dives in and strives to accomplish what I have called her to do. Her resolve is buoyed by my presence and encouragement.

Likewise, God wants us to trust him and his confidence in us. He has given us a high calling—to raise his children, with love and discipline. He knows that we can do this well if we choose to depend on him. This decision of dependence is a step of humility as we acknowledge our insufficiency and surrender to his all-sufficiency.

God has a course for our relationship with each of our children, which is intended to bless him, them, and us.

SURRENDER IS A STRENGTH

One afternoon I was overwhelmed by my inadequacies, discouraged by my seeming failures as a mom, and exhausted physically and emotionally. I collapsed to the sofa crying, and vented: *God, I am so frustrated! Nothing seems to be working. I don't feel like I'm doing anything right. I keep messing up as a mom, and I feel like a disappointment to you.*

After I emptied my heart and had a good cry, I sat subdued in silence—and clarity came. It dawned on me how I contribute to my exhaustion and experience of discouragement: Most days I try to be and do what *I* think a mom should be and do—without asking God to teach me, much less help me. I try to mold my children according to *my* goals, employing every ounce of *my* mental, emotional, and physical energy.

Humbled, I saw my pride. *God, I repent of my pride. I'm sorry for not inviting you to lead and help me. I need you.* What a relief to unload these thoughts and emotions to him, to know he forgives me, and to be able to start over—following God.

In those few minutes, my circumstance with the children did not change, but I felt like God was glad that I stopped and cried out to him. Focus on my failure shifted to hope in God. My perspective changed: I'm a mother *for* God. Therefore, I want to do this *his* way, *with him.* I recognize that I can't do this on my own; I need him.

All of this took only a few minutes. God knows how little time a mom has to be still, much less alone! From time to time, I pray this prayer when I recognize that my attitude is out of whack and I need to recommit my heart's path to God.

Practice: Prayer of Surrender and Dedication

1. Surrender each child by name to God:

   "God, I give you _____. She is your child whom you have given me for a season."

2. Claim and dedicate your relationship with each child to the God:

   "God, I claim my relationship with _____ for you. I dedicate this relationship to you. I want our relationship and how I parent _____ to glorify you. Amen."

Life circumstances will challenge our family. God hopes we will look to him for the way through. "Therefore, my beloved, as you have always obeyed, so now, not only as in my presence but much more in my absence, work out your own salvation with fear and trembling, for it is God who works in you, both to will and to work for his good pleasure" (Philippians 2:12–13). You are God's Beloved. Yield to his love and leadership.

In our culture, self-sufficiency is an ideal. If we make our own decisions, take care of ourself, and don't need anyone for anything, then we feel strong. God's kingdom on earth has an opposite ideal: All our needs are met in God. He wants us to seek his guidance for all decisions, to depend on him to take care of us, and to know we need him. In order to live this way, we need to surrender or release to God what we *want* to do—and then trust and obey him.

Surrender is really hard. Like all hard things, the more we practice, the better we get at it. Opportunity to practice occurs all day long. We lay down our preferred way for his: *God, I surrender _____ to you. Please help me discern and follow your way.*

Once we recognize surrender as a strength, desire to practice relying on God increases. It's humbling how quickly we can put ourself in the driver's seat with themes like training and correction methods, making plans, and relational issues. Sometimes our independent strategy works, but often we leave a trail of circumstances that needs to be rectified. Pray for grace and believe that God responds to your *effort* to yield. Gradually, our self-centered life is transformed to a Christ-centered life.

> For you formed my inward parts; you knitted me together in my mother's womb. I praise you, for I am fearfully and wonderfully made. Wonderful are your works; my soul knows it very well. My frame was not hidden from you, when I was being made in secret, intricately woven in the depths of the earth. Your eyes saw my unformed substance; in your book were written, every one of them, the days that were formed for me, when as yet there was none of them. (Psalm 139:13–16)

When we rely on God throughout the day, we trust that he knows us best and holds *the* plan for our life—including how to parent our child. God desires to parent us as he shows us how to parent our child.

To surrender is to trust God.

THINK ABOUT IT

1. Have you ever sought peace through a quick-fix solution?

   a. How long did your peace last?

2. Since becoming a mom, what personal freedom(s) do you miss?

   a. In a prayer, name these, give them to God, and ask for his comfort and peace.

3. What is your most recent big change?

   a. How can you benefit from releasing the former circumstance to God to embrace the new circumstance?

4. Name one thing that overwhelms you right now.

   a. What would you guess might be currently overwhelming your child?

   b. How might talking to God about your circumstance and your child's circumstance be helpful to each of you?

5. What do you tend to do when you feel inadequate as a mom?

   a. What does your child do when he feels inadequate?

6. Have you ever surrendered something you felt strongly about to God?

   a. How did that impact you?

2

More Than We Can Imagine

"PLEASE TELL ME IT gets easier!" I panted, as I shifted the baby from one hip to the other.

My friend paused and smiled, as though considering how to break it to me. "It doesn't really get easier. What we do just changes."

Hung like a conversation bubble over my head, her words followed me around the house for the next two days. Her answer was not what I expected or wanted to hear. *It has to get easier. Surely, this season is the hardest one of motherhood. If it's not, what am I going to do?*

With three children under age four, I often felt inadequate, exhausted, or disappointed in myself. I loved my children and their closeness in age, but I didn't like the way I was handling things. Daydreaming was my escape: *Life will be easier when . . .* My survival technique was to rationalize: *Just get through the twos . . . Potty training will be over one day . . . Learning to share cannot take forever . . .*

My friend's concise assessment of the pattern of parenthood was honest and realistic, not negative. Her intention was preparatory. For each child, when one stage nears its end, another stage begins to unfold. Practice appreciating the present: Return thanks to God daily, including the sweet *and* hard parts.

When things don't go the way we want or hope, when we feel inadequate or like a failure, it is tempting to wish the day or season away. Instead, call your season what it is—hard, daunting, exhausting, or discouraging. After you exhale that, take a deep breath and remember you are not meant to raise your child alone. Within ourself, we do not have the strength, patience, or love to give our child day in and day out. We lack wisdom to make decisions and resolve issues, and we need guidance for tomorrow. When we mess up, we need help to make amends. These are not criticisms, but cues that we need God.

God uniquely designed you, and he will build and fulfill his plan in and through you. Author of our days, God dwells with us in the present and knows what's around the corner. When we entrust our heart to him, he meets us where we are. In the quiet or craziness of the ordinary day, God grows our ability to learn to discern *him*. He responds to our effort and sheds insight about our character or our child's attitude or behavior. Today's practice prepares us for tomorrow. All that we learn in the current season strengthens us toward the next one.

What we need to know about being a mom and what we need to teach each child continually changes. We do not have to learn it all or know it all at once!

Here's a silly example for what I mean: Imagine your nine-year-old worries whether she will be a good driver, or she anxiously assumes other girls will be better drivers. What would you say to her? You want her to enjoy being nine. You know that being nine will have its own challenges. Plus, you have plans for her as a nine-year-old—helping her discover abilities she has, teaching her what she needs to know now, grounding her in how loved she is, inspiring her to dream, hope, and pray. You intend to develop and build her toward becoming ten, then eleven, and so on. *When* she needs to learn to drive, you will help her, because you want her to be a good driver.

Some of us wish or worry away the present and unfavorably imagine the future because we label ourself. For example, we observe a mother with older children and doubt our future ability to raise our child. Our prediction is based on who we are *today*. Slow down. Breathe. Be *here*. Live in the now and enjoy every morsel of God's grace. How we live the present affects our development and our attitude toward the future.

God created us to have relationship with him. An extension of this relationship is learning to partner with him to raise our child. Parenting is a part of our *walk* with God, so walk. Seek a holy rhythm in which you pursue God daily and trust that he will reveal each step to follow—as you need it. He does not make it hard. We do—when we take our eyes off him, decide to lead ourselves, or let anxiety rule our heart.

We want to be good moms, but wanting and trying are not enough. We cannot manufacture character traits like self-control, kindness, patience, wisdom, or discernment. God is the source of such attributes. Throughout the ordinary day and during the storms of life, he grows them in us, that we might reflect the character of Christ with our family. Each day presents building-block opportunities to seek God and practice following him. How we engage with him impacts our character development. As we participate with God in shaping our child's character, he simultaneously shapes ours.

CHARACTER

> She opens her mouth with wisdom, and the teaching of kindness is on her tongue. Her children rise up and call her blessed; her husband also, and he praises her: "Many women have done excellently, but you surpass them all."
> (Proverbs 31:26, 28–9)

Over the years I have watched many moms laugh softly as they hear these verses. Knowing ourself, we laugh, unable to imagine being *that* woman. The first time I read those verses I thought,

This sounds like a fairy tale. The children adore their mom, and the husband elevates her character above all other women. Really? It is very possible—for you. Scripture is God-breathed words. Every word is truth. It is hard to imagine becoming that woman because up to now our experience is the fruit of self-determination, self-expectation, and conflicting self-image conclusions. For a brief minute, we imagine trying to *make* ourself to become like her. We can't. God can mold us to become her.

The Message presents the same verses this way:

> When she speaks she has something worthwhile to say, and she always says it kindly . . . Her children respect and bless her; her husband joins in with words of praise: "Many women have done wonderful things, but you've outclassed them all!" (Proverbs 31:26, 28–9, MSG)

I want this. Don't you?

So how do we get there? One day at a time. Step up your relationship with God. Step aside and invite him to lead. Long ago as told throughout the Scriptures, God made and continues to make himself known to us. He helps us know him. As we deepen our communion with him, he overwhelms our soul with the truth and power of his love. Our desire heightens to participate with him as he builds us. When we identify and yield self-centered patterns, attitudes, and behaviors to God, he molds those places in our heart. Day by day, we learn to stop dwelling on what we cannot do and believe what he can do—in and through us.

SELF CONTROL

"I can't believe I said that. I tried so hard to keep my mouth closed. But I couldn't help it when . . ."

"I try not to yell. But when he does that, I just can't control myself."

Self-control is strength to manage our emotions, impulses, even our desires. We long for this. Self-control is measured when we are in the thick of whatever challenges us.

I have excellent self-control when there is no junk food in the house. But when chocolate or chips are in the pantry, the true measure of my self-control unfolds. Before you know it, I have eaten way more than my share *again*.

All of us want to be self-controlled with our children. We love them; we know they are *just kids*. Some days when the circumstances pile up, we somehow hold it together. The washing machine breaks, and we have four loads to do. We haven't had a good night's sleep in days. The rain is relentless, and all of us have cabin fever. The kids are arguing for the fourth day in a row. Even still, we manage—*until* One More Thing Happens. And we lose it—control of our emotions and maybe control of our behavior. We blame it on fatigue, the circumstances, or even the weather. Then we label ourself and our children: *I can't handle this! They are impossible!*

"But the fruit of the Spirit is love, joy, peace, patience, kindness, goodness, faithfulness, gentleness and self control" (Galatians 5:22–23a). Self-control is a *product* of a personal relationship with Jesus. Becoming self-controlled is a *process* of growth and transformation that God cultivates as we love him.

Consider a fruit-bearing tree: A wise farmer plants the tree and nurtures it. He knows a healthy, well-tended tree produces good fruit. God plants us. One large portion of our soil is our family. He nurtures and grows us as we engage with him in worship, prayer, and his Word. He transforms us through the power of his Holy Spirit and his character is *produced* in us—love, joy, peace, patience, kindness, goodness, faithfulness, gentleness, and *self-control*.

> Blessed is the man who trusts in the LORD, whose trust is the LORD. He is like a tree planted by water, that sends out its roots by the stream, and does not fear when heat comes, for its leaves remain green, and is not anxious in the year of drought, for it does not cease to bear fruit. (Jeremiah 17:7–8)

One week I felt like I was regressing, not progressing. I was impatient and raised my voice every day. *God, I'm frustrated. I pray and read my Bible, but I don't feel like I am changing much.* That night, God gave me clarity. Reflecting about recent weeks, I realized how little I talk to him throughout the day. I bookend the day with him and do what I feel like in the middle. Thankfully, God loves us through our life lessons. We learn from our mistakes, our leaves remain green, and fruit grows.

Jesus describes how to have the relationship with him that God created us to enjoy:

> Abide in me, and I in you. As the branch cannot bear fruit by itself, unless it abides in the vine, neither can you, unless you abide in me. I am the vine; you are the branches. Whoever abides in me and I in him, he it is that bears much fruit, for apart from me you can do nothing. (John 15:4-5)

Jesus wants us to understand the significance of abiding in him. To abide is to be present to his presence—wherever you are, whatever you are doing. Some of us abide with our mobile phone. We're present to it *while* we do all sorts of other things—at work, spending time with a child, driving, watching a soccer match, cooking supper, or even having a conversation with someone. Imagine if we abided with Jesus this way—sharing our thoughts and listening to his.

Abiding—or not—affects the condition of our heart. Our heart is either bent toward ourself or bent toward God. Our bent or focus influences our degree of self-control. For example: We are already exhausted, but then our teenager or toddler yells at us in public. The condition of our heart affects whether we react or respond to the child.

We *react* when our focus is ourself—how the situation makes *us* look and how *our* agenda is affected. Every emotion that wells up in us fuels what we say or do next. We *give* the child what we *feel* in the moment. We lose our temper, say something we later regret, or we manipulate. God is with us in those minutes, but we are *not* present to him.

We *respond* when our focus is God: In the heat of the moment we wrestle with anger, hurt, and discouragement, yet we depend on our Partner to attend the struggle he sees in our heart.

Our effort blesses him. He moves in our heart and molds us to *participate* with him in the moment. Those minutes are still hard because we are human, but God carries us *through* them.

Countless times my thoughts prior to a conversation with a child were judgmental or critical. Or, in the heat of a stressful situation, retaliatory remarks burned in me. But in the hours or days leading up to the conversation, *and* during the conversation, I would give God my struggle and feelings and ask for his help. Every time I did this, I was amazed by the outcome, including my words and behavior. *Wow, I can't believe something that positive came out of my mouth, because I know what I was thinking before our conversation.* God works in us from the inside out, transforming our ugly to beauty.

It is not magic. It's the power of God, moving mountains in our heart.

We work at knowing him. We relinquish our old ways and clear space in our heart for him. He builds us new. God's power is made perfect in our weakness. That's amazing grace.

We can become healthy responders. Jesus is our Redeemer, and he can rebuild our relationship with a child.

Practice: Prayer to Address Reacting

1. Invite God to reveal patterns and examples: "God, expose my patterns of reacting. Help me recognize when I'm reacting." Some may be evident quickly. Others may be revealed in circumstances.

2. Name and release each to God.

3. Pray for healing: "Please heal my child where I've hurt or confused him when I react." If specific memories come to mind, ask God to heal each place.

4. Pray for the relationship: "Please heal our relationship."

WISDOM

"I've read so many parenting books that I don't know what to believe any more." My friend was frustrated. She didn't have a good role model growing up, and she wanted to be a good mom. Books were her compass. "I wish I had known to go to God about all this." Invariably, we seek tangible resources first. When we are at our wit's end, we cry to God as our last resort. My friend believed in God, but it was a new concept to consider God as her primary guide for parenting.

"If any of you lacks wisdom, you should ask God, who gives generously to all without finding fault, and it will be given to you" (James 1:5, NIV). God is the source of wisdom. Be a recipient of his generous pour.

When we think, decide, act, or struggle alone, we ignore a storehouse of perfect wisdom:

I need a sounding board, someone to talk to about this. God listens.

I feel like I'm carrying the weight of this decision by myself. He wants to carry your burden, but waits for you to give it to him and invite his help.

I wish someone would just tell me what to do. God will lead you forward.

Pray. Ask for wisdom. Listen and wait expectantly. God responds to a sincere heart and gives his wisdom, knowledge, and understanding.

> For the LORD gives wisdom; from his mouth come knowledge and understanding; he stores up sound wisdom for the upright; he is a shield to those who walk in integrity, guarding the paths of justice and watching over the way of his saints. Then you will understand righteousness and justice and equity, every good path; for wisdom will come into your heart, and knowledge will be pleasant to your soul; discretion will watch over you; understanding will guard you. (Proverbs 2:6–11)

DISCERNMENT AND GUIDANCE

"Then I saw and considered it; I looked and I received instruction" (Proverbs 24:32).

When we consider, we pause and invite space. Thinking is important. Prayer is powerful. As we invite God in, he leads us to discern the root cause and imparts insight. Not taking time to consider, we may act impulsively. Try this prayer exercise to consider with God the way forward for your circumstance.

Practice: Learning to Consider with God

1. Invite God's guidance: "God, help me address my daughter's whining."

2. Spend time considering the problem: "Please show me what I need to know or see."

3. Ask specific questions: "What do I need to do or stop doing? How should I work with her through this?"

4. Pray for God to move in both hearts: "Please change this in her. Help me learn what you want me to learn."

PEACE FOR THE PRESENT

"They grow up so fast." Whenever someone said this to me, I paused for a second, thinking, *I should probably appreciate her well-intended words*. But silently I reacted, *Right now, it's not going fast enough*. Days can be long. Hard seasons feel endless.

Mothers on the other side of our current season look in their rearview mirror of motherhood and the details of their former seasons blur. They bear witness that children *do* grow up—and we grow with them.

From the best days to the hardest, God bonds our heart with each child's heart. He supplies all that we need *even when we don't ask*. Looking back even now, we can see much that God has done—in our child and in us. We can mark his allowances and protection, his grace and mercy. Gratitude swells for all that he has helped us do up to this point—things that we never *imagined* we could do.

As time distances us from prior stages, we realize how short each really was. On the larger canvas of life, each stage blends into the next. Each brush stroke has purpose, for the child and for us. Memories of hard experiences slowly fade as love covers all.

Treasure *now*. Soak up what God has for your child and you *now*. Don't wish or worry it away. They grow up so fast.

THINK ABOUT IT

1. Does the idea of partnering with God to raise your child comfort you?

   a. What do you think is necessary for this to be a true partnership?

2. Which describes you most, and consider why:

   a. I embrace the season I'm in.

   b. I wish away the season I'm in.

3. Proverbs 31 describes a woman whose character has been shaped through her relationship with God.

   a. Do you recognize traits in you that God is shaping?

   b. How do you think God uses your child and your circumstances for some of your shaping?

4. If self-control is a product of cultivating a personal relationship with Jesus, what steps could you take toward this?

5. Sometimes we react and other times we respond to our child.

   a. When do you tend to react, and when do you tend to respond?

   b. Pray about your insights.

3

Finding Rhythm

WHEN MY CHILDREN WERE very young, I spent too many hours fretting that I didn't have balance in my life. My time—which no longer felt like *my* time—was nowhere near evenly distributed among categories like exercise, time with friends, time for myself, Bible study, time with my husband, and rest. Several of those categories were hit or miss weekly.

After yet another day of stressing over this, I put pursuit of balance on the shelf and decided to pursue a daily rhythm.

Rhythm is pattern and flow. It's not the same thing as a schedule, but schedule fits into our rhythm. The beauty of rhythm is that it can be as unique as we are. We can identify a design for rhythm that works for us and works for our home, that settles peace in our heart—even when the day is crazy busy or discouragingly hard.

Our rhythm can have variety or change temporarily. For instance, our rhythm on the weekend is likely different from the rhythm of a school day, or the rhythm of our day off is different from the days we work. Circumstances can affect rhythm. When we move to a new city, our rhythm is altered until we are settled. A job change, a new extracurricular activity for a child, or a new special-needs circumstance for a child or aging parent make modifications necessary.

A healthy rhythm reflects attention to our sense of personal order, how we plan, how we communicate, flexibility, and enjoying our life.

Our day is unpredictable *to us*, but never to God. No matter what comes, his peace can anchor us. How we live the day affects our antennae for God's peace. Cultivating rhythm—pattern and flow—helps.

ORDER

Some love it. Others loathe it. The rest of us often feel defeated trying to gain it. Where are you on the scale of Perfectionism to Perfectly Happy with Messy (*If I organize it, I won't know where anything is*)? Largely influenced by our experiences, definition and desire for order varies widely.

Then there's God's view. In the Old Testament, God demonstrates he is a God of order through details of creation, the Ten Commandments, the building of temples, and procedures for sacrifice. He continues in the New Testament with the ordering of spiritual gifts and the distribution of them in the body so that his church is built up. The Bible provides pattern for how we are to live the day and live in relationship with each other.

We follow God's lead. His design for you will bless you and those you love. When we independently define what order looks like for us, we miss God's best for how he intends to help us live each day. It's also likely that we eventually frustrate others and ourself. In a home, each member's approach to order may be different, but if we each pursue God's definition, harmonious understanding will cover our differences.

One day I noticed how frequently I straightened the sofa pillows, which was humorous considering I had three very active small children. *This is ridiculous; I am stressing myself out!* As I walked through the room, I asked God to show me other ways that I generated my own stress. This led to a huge personal breakthrough. I identified unrealistic expectations I placed on myself concerning our home and recalled perfectionistic patterns instilled in me growing up. Some of my patterns about order were easy to lay down, and others had layers that God has revealed over time through circumstances. Contentedness has replaced the stress I carried around for so long.

Practice: Identify Unhealthy Patterns

1. Invite God to show you: "Lord, I want to come to order in your way that is best for me. Please show me my unhealthy patterns of being ordered or disordered."

2. Be still, quiet, and wait. Patterns that generate stress or conflict tend to be our unhealthy patterns. As things come to mind, talk to God about each: "My kitchen has to be spotless." "I forget to pay the bills."

3. Release each to God: "I give this pattern to you."

4. Ask for insight about self-expectations: "Please show me my self-expectations about order." Give these to God.

5. Ask God for help: "I invite you to have this place in my heart. Please teach me your way and empower me to change. Thank you."

Some patterns take time to undo or establish. The apostle Paul gives testimony that as we admit our struggle and seek the power of Jesus, he meets us with his power and grace.

> He [the Lord] said to me, "My grace is sufficient for you, for my power is made perfect in weakness." Therefore I [Paul] will boast all the more gladly of my weaknesses, so that the power of Christ may rest upon me. For the sake of Christ, then, I am content with weaknesses . . . For when I am weak, then I am strong. (2 Corinthians 12:9–10)

Our children learn from our patterns, just as we have learned from our parents. Some patterns are intentionally taught and others are observed. God leads us toward healthy patterns for order and shows us how to help our children learn patterns that will serve them well. Living into God's design for order yields peace.

PLAN

"Commit your work to the LORD, and your plans will be established" (Proverbs 16:3).

Everyone plans. We plan to *not* have a plan or we plan everything. God instructs us to entrust our work for each day to him. He promises that when we do he will establish our plans. He will settle in our heart his way forward for the day. This could be the plans that we already intended or ones quite different. One thing is certain: All of it will work together for his good.

God gives us generous quantities of time. We can waste it or worship him through it. Each time we yield it, our heart worships God as *Lord* of our life. As we entrust *to* him, God grows our trust *in* him. In the crazy, busy days or the hard, discouraging days, we begin to recognize how lovingly near to us God is. Our understanding for his design for a day increases. We enjoy his pleasure in moments markedly his—a conversation that occurs through the unfolding of particular events, a doctor appointment that seems to fit perfectly within a day of unexpected changes, or an unforeseen window of alone time with a child.

List makers, surrender that list every morning. Pray: *God, here is what I think I need to do today and what I want to do today. Please help me discern which items, if any, on this list are for today.* Making a list helps us organize. If we race against the clock and tackle every obstacle to savor an accomplished to-do list, our satisfaction is short-lived. It does not compare to the sustaining peace that God pours into our heart when we attempt to trust his leading instead.

Go-with-the-flow types, surrender daily the tendency to follow your feelings. Pray: *God, here's what I feel like doing. Please order my pace and steps.* Seek the flow of the Holy Spirit. God's structure for us matches the deepest yearnings within our heart. Align with his pace and enjoy his blessing.

Whether you make lists, go with the flow, or describe yourself somewhere in between these, ask yourself: *Who do I intend to serve today?* When we determine to follow our list or follow our feelings, we aim to serve ourself. When we entrust the day to God, we serve him.

"Look carefully then how you walk, not as unwise but as wise, making the best use of the time, because the days are evil. Therefore do not be foolish, but understand what the will of the Lord is" (Ephesians 5:15–17). He helps us identify our foolish ways and learn his wise way. We practice and learn as God leads and empowers us.

He teaches us to discern the unnecessary and reveals how to accomplish the necessary. With practice, we learn to pause during the day to see how God leads. His peace that passes understanding redefines our personal satisfaction. Our to-do list may go untouched because we seem led to do other things, like call a friend or sit on the floor and play with our kids. We discover that doing something because we feel *led* to, rather than because we *want* to, gratifies our heart.

Lastly, have you ever felt like you are a victim of your day? When we plan, we're more likely to be the master of the day. "She rises while it is yet night and provides food for her household and portions for her maidens" (Proverbs 31:15). Rise early and prepare. Think through supper, errands, family members' schedules, homework, and potential time with one another. When the unforeseen occurs, we can wrap ourself in God's presence and trust him to lead us through. His peace, rather than panic, clothes our heart even as the hard day unfolds.

COMMUNICATE

"That would have been nice to know."

"Why didn't you tell me?"

Our child says this. We say it too. Poor communication breeds frustration and strains our relationship with our child. Thoughtful and intentional communication demonstrates consideration and builds relationship.

We don't owe our child an itinerary. His plans don't supersede ours. Yet, sometimes we inflict our plan on a child and wonder why he reacts with attitude: "You'll have to finish that later. You have a dental appointment today. Go brush your teeth." What our child is doing at that time matters to him. Our abrupt interruption conveys indifference. Thoughtful preparation displays respect: "Supper will be ready in fifteen minutes, so finish up whatever you're doing."

It's natural for a child to whine or complain when he doesn't like the plan he hears. Pray for grace for him in these moments, that he'll grow to accept and respect our direction. As a child experiences consideration, he learns how to be considerate and respectful. Treat your child the way that you want to be treated. How we communicate instructs the child for how to communicate with us.

When our children were little, they met me with a succession of questions first thing in the morning: "What are we doing today? Can we go to the park?" Though much of what we do is done in front of our children, they don't naturally pay attention to our activities. To them, our activities are like background music. One day in simple language I told the children about some of my responsibilities and their importance—things like doing the laundry and cooking. Our children have no reason to appreciate these things until we inform them.

Likewise, when a child asks, give a response that helps the child and ends the question: "Not today. I need to finish something to take to work tomorrow." The child might not like our answer, but she experiences consideration as we explain. Pray God's peace for her heart. A simple no is fine, but it invites the follow-up question that raises our stress level: "Why not?"

The Family Calendar

A family calendar presents us with a month-by-month overview of life in our family. Family events plus each member's schedule tell the story of a day, a week, or a month. This helps us plan, and it prepares us for heavy and light days. It also signals when one person or the family as a whole is too busy.

Keep a large family calendar in the kitchen where everyone can see plans for the whole family and individual schedules. Family unity builds as each member feels informed about the overall family schedule. Children become aware of each other's activities.

We lead well, demonstrate thoughtfulness, and avoid stressful dialogue when we keep our children informed as to what is going on within the family. When the calendar is particularly full, run through the day's events at breakfast. Children are prepared for things they don't want to do, like go to a sibling's practice. An overview helps them set realistic expectations—of us, and about what they will or will not be able to do that day or that week. For example, when our daughter learns that her sister has a soccer game, she knows not to ask us to take her shopping after school.

A brief reminder at supper preps children for the next day and often triggers a child's memory to recall a forgotten event or time change that will impact the family: "I forgot that I need to go to school early tomorrow to get extra help in math before the test." This provides enough notice to work out a new plan.

Frequent communication lessens unnecessary stress.

Routines and Boundaries

Establish routines and clear boundaries. When these two structures are in place, children feel secure. They feel prepared and know what to expect. Study each, determine what works well, and stick with it.

Routines tend to involve segments of the day like morning hygiene, daily chores, after school, and getting ready for bed. Clearly stated guidelines help a child understand what's expected and adjust. Any challenge to our authority eventually weakens when we hold to our plan. For example, when our children were in elementary school, they'd come home from school, have a healthy snack, and get straight to their homework so that they could then go outside to play. This didn't happen overnight. After a few weeks of complaining and challenging me, they learned that I meant what I said. The after school routine became the accepted norm.

Unspoken or inconsistent expectations invite confusion. Determine what you want your child to be responsible for and make this clear. For example, on weekends, holidays, or during the summer, a child knows that he has to finish his chores before he goes out to play. When a friend knocks on the door or calls, your child can confidently respond. Also, make guidelines for activities clear. For instance, what, if any, television can your child watch during the week? When is bedtime? Can an older child go out during the school week?

Children like choices. Keep it to two. If your ten-year-old has a friend spend the night, predetermine the time they have to quiet down and start going to sleep. If she begs for more time, give her a choice. For example, "I said 11:00 before your friend arrived. You choose—10:30 or 11:00." If dressing becomes a daily drama, set apart time to listen to the child's struggle. Then provide a couple of options for how she can determine her outfit each day. Help her try each option to then decide which works for her.

Review routines and boundaries with children frequently, until they demonstrate a cooperative rhythm. This is draining, but worthwhile in the end. Repetition benefits children and alleviates stress for us. When our three children were little, going shopping quickly became a high-stress ordeal. After one particularly draining grocery store adventure, I made a plan. Before we entered any store, I reviewed with the children where each child was to sit in or on the shopping buggy. After they repeated it back to me, we reviewed our store rules:

"Are we getting a treat in the check out line?"

"No."

"How many cookies do you get at the bakery?"

"One."

Our trips became pleasant, and eventually the children became my helpers.

With older kids, restate or ask them to state the boundaries for the situation. For example, "What time do you have to be home?" "If your plans change, what do you do?" Review greatly reduces the potential for misbehavior and increases the probability that we can praise their behavior later.

When we establish routines and fair boundaries, we lead our children. We present the way forward to help each child learn healthy rhythm.

FLEXIBILITY

Life can be full of interruptions, emergencies, and little crises. For a mom, there are so many more because our children will *initiate* interruptions, *require* emergency attention, and *instigate* little crises, individually and with their siblings. In the midst of days when nothing is going our way and our plans are disintegrating before our eyes, God shapes a valuable trait—flexibility.

A story: The day begins quietly. I manage to secure a sweet fifteen minutes reading my Bible, and I feel strong and ready to seize the day. A general plan settles in my mind. Next, I wake the children with hugs and head downstairs to prepare breakfast. Twenty minutes later, I hear two of the kids bickering upstairs, which means they aren't getting dressed for school. Another child complains throughout breakfast. Finally, we're in the car, but one remembers he forgot his project, so back in the house I go. When I drive away from the school, I exhale as though I just ran an obstacle course. *I'm exhausted and the day has just gotten started.* Before 9:00 a.m., all semblance of peace evaporated from my body. What happened?

When the day turns upside down, a crossroads emerges. We can suppress our emotions, sink into them, or follow the *new* direction that God presents. Often we grip our plan, we press on. *I am not going to let this get to me.* Mentally, we step over the unwelcome unexpected and keep moving. Suppressed feelings in tow, we inevitably erupt *onto* an innocent someone or *about* something insignificant. On the other hand, giving in to our emotions seldom ends well either. For example, if we allow discouragement to sink in, we're tempted to wallow in self-pity and waste the day. Permitting anger its course, our attitude is tainted toward everyone and about everything. By day's end, we've dug a large hole of regret.

If we pray, plan, and commit our day to God, shouldn't this formula produce a peaceful *day*? Jesus prepares us that in this life we will face trials. Yet, in the *midst* of everything or everyone falling apart—or nothing coming together—God is with us. When we hold on to him *in the midst* of the crazy, we discover his peace prevails.

"Peace I leave with you; my peace I give to you. Not as the world gives do I give to you. Let not your hearts be troubled, neither let them be afraid" (John 14:27). Jesus assures his disciples that the peace he gives is stronger that all our circumstances and worries. No one can take away the peace that he gives us. However, we have to decide to take our eyes off our circumstance and focus them on him, the Prince of Peace.

Flexibility is willingness to adjust. Some adjustments are hard, discouraging, and even hurtful. Here are four simple steps to invite God to tend our heart and lead us through whatever adjustment is necessary:

Practice: Prayer for Flexibility

1. Describe and give God your emotions: "I give my frustration and disappointment to you. I really wanted to go _____."

2. Forgive: "I choose to forgive _____ for _____." This step is helpful when you feel offended.

3. Seek God's forgiveness if necessary: "I lost my temper when _____. I'm sorry and ask your forgiveness."

4. Invite God's guidance and help: "Show me how to order my day now. Please comfort me and help my perspective. I trust your plan."

Expect Interruptions!

One summer, my husband and I were invited to serve at a Christian girl's camp. Before going, a wise friend advised, "Remember, much ministry happens in the interruptions—the time in between the planned activities." His words inspired us to be alert. We were amazed as God presented opportunities when we walked between activities, did laundry, cleaned tables after a meal, or checked our mailbox. Comfortable in the ordinary, counselors unloaded burdens and listened eagerly for direction. Each day God provided the setting for us to participate with him as he tended the hearts of these young people.

When we read the Gospel accounts, we see that people often interrupted Jesus. They asked questions, challenged things he said, or they wanted something of him. Sometimes Jesus seized the moment of interruption and amazed everyone with his response or miraculous healing. On other occasions, Jesus did not tarry. He stayed his course—to journey to the next town, to go pray alone, or to rest with his disciples. In other words, he discerned when God wanted him to stop to be attentive to someone and when to continue on, not permitting the interruption to delay his plan.

Interruptions abound in our homes. Imagine the possibilities with our transformed view. As we make dinner, work on a project, or read, a child might approach to ask a question, vent, or share a random thought or significant experience. At other times a child wants companionship, so she asks what we're doing or tries to pull us toward what she wants to do. We might be interrupted multiple times within minutes. So, how are we to handle this? None of us want to miss God's moments. Regrettably, some of my uglier moments include how I have mishandled a child's interruption.

It's important to teach children manners for how and when to interrupt, and we need to practice patience as they learn. At the same time, we need to be available to them. Our kids are not supposed to make appointments with us. They can't predict the questions they'll have in an hour or when a circumstance will generate stress or when they're going to want to share what happened at school. They speak when the matter surfaces. Isn't this better than not speaking at all?

Don't miss this: Your child decided to come to *you*. Taking this privilege for granted could one day turn the child away. If our behavior communicates that we don't have time for our child, he may go elsewhere—to a friend, another adult, a stranger in cyber space—to someone who gives him attention. In hindsight, countless parents would be grateful for an interruption from their child today—to experience their child initiate desire to engage in conversation.

When we are preoccupied, too busy, or too tired, we heighten the probability that we will miss opportune interruptions in which God has purpose. I learned this the hard way during a season when I was managing several projects. While I worked at the computer, the kids frequently approached me with questions. Initially, I paused to be present to them, but gradually I answered without even a glance. I became singularly focused on my agenda and insensitive to three precious children. Then God got my attention.

One day my ten-year-old son approached, "Mom . . ." I cut in annoyed, "What?" Not turning my head toward him, still staring at the computer screen, I heard a dispirited, "Never mind." I looked up from the computer and saw his face as he turned to leave. Suddenly, the significance of my work evaporated. *I hurt him. He is ashamed that he bothered me or discouraged that I was too busy for him.* That experience was a wake-up call for me.

Children interrupt us with challenges, questions, needs, and desire for companionship. Most interruptions last only a few minutes and are unique opportunities to gain insight about a child, to demonstrate interest in him, and to build our relationship. Once we consider that many interruptions are not disruptions, our heart opens to God's prompts to seize more moments. We learn to pause to discern what he wants us to see, say, do—or stop doing.

LAUGH

"Strength and dignity are her clothing, and she laughs at the time to come" (Proverbs 31:25). Blend the seriousness of life with pleasure. Enjoy God's grace and delight to extend it to your children. Welcome the lightness of laughter to your heart. Let the joy of the Lord be your strength. There are times to be serious with them—and times to laugh and enjoy one another.

At times we're so determined to accomplish a goal that we miss great moments for laughter. When one of our boys was two, he attempted to eat lettuce with his spoon. Delighted that he was trying, I encouraged him. Inches from his mouth, the lettuce fell from his spoon every time. Clearly wanting to please, he persevered. After watching him open his mouth wide several times only to have the lettuce drop just before reaching his mouth, I got the giggles. The circumstance became preciously funny to me. Not wanting him to think I was laughing at *him*, I said, "You're trying so hard, but that lettuce just won't stay on your spoon!" He gave me a big smile, put down his spoon, threw his little head back, and giggled uncontrollably.

Then there are those it's-not-appropriate-to-laugh-now circumstances. On one such occasion my children and I were in a worship service. Often we sat in the second row because their daddy was up front preaching. I am confident we entertained those sitting behind us, especially one day: I was training the children to not talk during the message. Four-year-old Ellison was determined to get my attention *during* the message. Seated two seats over from me, he tried whispering loudly, tugging on my sleeve, and leaning forward to stare at me. Aware of his efforts, I continued to look forward as though I was listening to the preacher, though I had not heard a word. Ellison's determination to turn my head matched my determination to hold firm and establish my new rule.

Minutes of quiet passed. *Whew, he got the message.* I exhaled relief too soon. Within seconds, Ellison stood in front of me, his face inches in front of mine. He cupped my face and whispered loudly, "Mommy, look at me!" Those big brown determined eyes melted my resolve. His loud effort to be quiet was adorable and hilarious, and I could not stop giggling. I scooped Ellison into my lap, hugged him close, and counted down the minutes for the message to end.

Laughter softens our perspective, especially when we get too serious. As we teach and train, give place for laughter. This can reduce stress and enable us to address our child with grace and fairness. Pray for joy in your home and in your heart.

Laugh at yourself. Don't pretend to be a know-it-all. Be genuine. When my children started roller-blading, I bought myself a pair of skates. *I loved to roller-skate when I was a child. This can't be much different.* I quickly discovered that they made it look easier than it was. Through their giggles, my kids tried to encourage me, but I got frustrated with myself.

My pride almost ruined the afternoon. Determined to master the skates, I became hardly aware of the children. Then I looked up at their faces. Staring at me, their smiles were gone and they looked confused, almost somber. Regret consumed my heart. Trying hard not to fall, I realized the absurdness of my seriousness and how silly I probably looked. I burst out laughing and so did they. Then our fun began, even though it was mostly at my expense.

Fun and laughter are building blocks for rich relationship. God wants us to live as children at heart. Enjoy your children. Laugh *with* them. Get into their fun. Relax and look at life through their eyes sometimes. Discover what makes them giggle. Is it a cartoon character, a comic strip, corny jokes, silly circumstances, or random things that happen in a day?

"The cheerful of heart has a continual feast" (Proverbs 15:15b).

THINK ABOUT IT

1. How would you describe yourself: perfectionist, taskmaster, somewhat orderly, organized in my own way, very disorganized?

   a. Do you like the way you operate or would you like to modify it?

   b. Does your method stress you and/or your family?

2. Do you tend to communicate a plan to your child or insert her into it?

   a. What is your child's response?

   b. Does your child tend to communicate like you?

3. Establishing routines and clear boundaries can be challenging.

   a. Do you have a routine that currently helps your child and you?

   b. What other aspect of your day or your child's day could benefit from a routine?

   c. What is the most challenging boundary for you to maintain?

4. Do you tend to *react* or *respond* to your child's interruptions?

   a. Consider some tender interruptions you have experienced.

5. How have you trained your child to interrupt politely?

6. Reflect on a time, involving your child, where the *unexpected* release of laughter is a special memory.

4

Beyond Survival

DID YOU EVER IMAGINE that juggling would be in your skill set? *And* you're better at it than you may think. Managing the home, the family, school, yourself, and possibly employment is a lot. Breaking it down, we oversee everyone's activities, health, and development on various levels. Our children have needs and wants; our husband has needs and wants; we have needs and wants. Add to this the time spent wrestling with what we think we should do, what others tell us we should or could do, and what we don't want to do.

That's a lot to juggle, mentally and physically. The potential for stress and relational upheaval hangs in the balance. To help maintain peace in our home and in our heart, weave the following practices into your rhythm.

EMBRACE EACH SEASON

In his sovereignty, God has allowed or designed our current season. Lovingly and purposefully, he reigns over it. Relationship problems, financial issues, loneliness, workload, or health concerns can usher in a season of uncertainty and tension. Before this, the everyday stress was manageable, but our new circumstance overwhelms us. God knows exactly what is happening. Hold on to him tightly and step in to the work he is doing. Engage with him, cry out for help, and listen for his leading.

Endurance is hard work. Willingness to trust God is an essential muscle. "She . . . works with willing hands" (Proverbs 31:13b). Without willingness, our heart hardens. Complaining, negativity, or rebellion set in. When we are willing, we lower the guard over our heart and open it to God. We welcome his stretching and shaping to receive all that he wills to do in and through us during this hard season.

"Charm is deceitful, and beauty is vain, but a woman who fears the Lord is to be praised" (Proverbs 31:30). In our culture, charm and beauty get a lot of attention, as we give countless hours of focus toward our appearance. God edifies the woman who honors him with a yielded heart. This woman seeks daily to discern and obey his will. As she does, her heart's beauty bursts through to her outer self, and she reflects the love of Christ. Hmm, that is truly beautiful—and lasting.

When I was six months pregnant with our second child, I was diagnosed with sciatica. The baby rested on a nerve in my lower back. Around the same time, my husband began a new job and we bought our first house. In a short span of time, I stepped into several new seasons! Unfortunately, this revelation didn't occur to me.

Stubbornly, I determined to unpack our boxes and complete several projects in our new home before Baby No. 2 arrived. One day while unpacking a box, I had a meltdown. The constant excruciating pain in my back caused me to take three times as long to do anything. The physical, mental, and emotional toll heaped discouragement on my weary soul. I sank into a nearby chair and burst into tears. Angry and full of self-pity, I softly cried, "I don't get it, God. Why won't you heal me? You know all that's going on in our life. I've got to get us settled!" I knew my attitude was way out of joint, but I just sat there. Pouting.

After a few minutes, I went and got my Bible, hoping I could read something to help me. I had no idea where to turn, which worsened my mood. "God, I don't know where to turn for how I feel." More minutes passed, and the book of James came to mind. I turned there and began to read. I didn't need to go very far. "Count it all joy, my brothers, when you meet trials of various kinds, for you know that the testing of your faith produces steadfastness" (James 1:2–3). Holding on to my sour attitude, I thought, *Well, I am clearly in a trial, but I don't see anything to be joyful about.*

Then our son Terrell, who had recently turned one, made a sound. All morning, he played with his toys quietly nearby. This was not the first day I had taken advantage of his easy manner to accomplish my goals. It was a humbling moment.

Looking at my little boy, who was really still a baby, my heart surged with love and gratitude for him. God knew my child was unknowingly content being in the room with his mommy. Yet, I knew how much more rich the hours could have been for him, and this grieved my heart. God was exposing the joy in my trial.

I had ignored the doctor's advice to sit more and take it easy because I was determined to have my way. Now I saw the blessings of my limitations. For the remaining three months, my joy in this trial was to focus on Terrell and demonstrate how much I love him before our next baby arrived. Had I continued my agenda, the home would be settled, but sadly Terrell and I would have missed a special time that God knew we needed.

Two more "joys" unfolded. The power of my stubbornness humbled me. I was motivated to shed this trait and asked God to help me and change me. Also, because I had sciatica, I rested more than I would have otherwise. God was taking care of me and protecting our unborn baby. The unpacking would get done—in God's timing.

What happens when we try to manipulate the season we're in? Can we pull it off? Probably. But someone will suffer—our husband, one of the children, a parent/child relationship, or us. We can miss God's best when we are convinced *we* know what is best.

A friend of mine delights to share her artistic gift with others, especially with her church. They would ask her to lead projects that involved art, and she seldom said no because she enjoyed the projects and the people. She had two little girls, ages two and five.

One afternoon she told me that she was going to step down from all her involvements. Sadly yet peacefully, she explained, "I teach and spend time with everyone but my own children. Even when I am home, I'm working on a project or thinking about it."

To lay it all down was a sacrifice for her; she was visibly grieving. At the same time, she felt that she was sacrificing time with her children for her own pleasure and to please others. She understood that her artistic gifts were from God, so she trusted that he would reveal the season to enjoy her gift with others again. Right then she looked forward to enjoying her gift with her girls.

LEARN TO DELEGATE

If we do all the work, we *train* our children not to work. When we teach them how to help and serve within the family, we train them to be contributors. Children benefit from having responsibilities, learning to work together, and helping each other.

As each of our children turned three, I gave them the responsibility to make their own bed by pulling the covers to the top of the bed. It was a cute sight. Sitting on the bed, facing the covers of the unmade bed, the child grabs the covers and scoots backward until he pulls the covers over the pillow. Lumps don't matter. Over time their skills improve, as should our standards. "The path of lazy people is overgrown with briers; the diligent walk down a smooth road" (Proverbs 15:19, MSG).

As children get older, their responsibilities should increase. Around the age of eight, chores can be distinguished by two categories—personal and household. Personal responsibilities include maintaining their bedroom and bathroom. The description of these responsibilities can be modified each year according to the child's age and ability. For example, an eight-year-old can hang her towel and tidy items around the sink. Household chores include things like sweeping, setting the table, or feeding a pet. Our children learn life skills and responsibility, and our workload is lightened.

Another way to delegate is to include the children in larger, occasional chores like washing the car, yard work, or cleaning out the garage. We are training them to work alongside each other. Seize opportunities to encourage each child for his helpfulness, ideas, or some other strength we notice as we work together. When a family works together, children gain a sense of unity, which strengthens their self-esteem and contributes to harmony.

TAKE TIME FOR SELF

Did you laugh or roll your eyes when you read the title? When our children were babies and toddlers, I laughed at this idea because I felt like I needed every minute to merely cover the essential bases for the present day. If I had a babysitter or the children were in preschool, I used that time to run errands. As the children got older, their needs and my commitments spread. When I went back to work, my time was further divided between family and work needs. When anyone suggested I take some time for myself, I rolled my eyes because I couldn't imagine where that time existed.

"Come to me, all who labor and are heavy laden, and I will give you rest" (Matthew 11:28). God gives rest. He invites us to come to him for restoration. Take at least a few minutes a day to sit, pray, and receive from him: *God, I'm tired. I need you. Please fill and restore me now and help me complete this day. Thank you.*

Faithfully, God provides time for us to breathe—to relax, rest, and even play. Take time to unload to him what holds you back from receiving personal time that he has prepared for you. He knows the best time for each of us to *take* time for ourself. Ask him. What he has for you will satisfy you for this particular season in your life.

To give our best to those we love most, we need to take care of ourself. Personal neglect benefits no one.

EVALUATE

Imagine if dentists, teachers, or doctors seldom evaluated their procedures or effectiveness. What if they never examined the impact of their manner on their people group?

Evaluation refines. Forge this practice into your rhythm.

Periodically evaluate components that infuse daily living. Take time to consider themes like individual relationships, health, work, and time usage. To avoid an avalanche of overwhelm, tackle one theme at a time. Invite God into the process. He helps us see the overall present picture and then gently reveals what we need to know for now. Sometimes we might be surprised. *Why didn't I see that before? What was I thinking?* Other times God confirms our thoughts. *Thank you, Lord, for a sense of peace about my job; you know I doubted my decision.* Or, *Wow, it really does make a difference when I'm in the room while he does his homework. Thank you for getting my attention about that.*

God sees when we want to improve. He responds and molds our heart.

Practice: Evaluate with God

- "God, I lift my relationship with _____ to you. As we enter a new season, help me see her the way I need to. Show me ways to spend time with her."

- "I haven't exercised in months. Please show me what is reasonable in this season."

- "Lord, I'm bringing too much work home, and I need your help to stop. Please show me healthy boundaries."

- "I want to be a good steward of the time you give me. Please show me where I waste time. Show me any activities I need to step away from."

Evaluate each child's activities, time usage, and relationships occasionally. This removes potential tensions for the child, our relationship, and us. To be faithful stewards of our children, we partner with the One who gave them to us. God has the panoramic view and the master plan. Our view is limited and easily influenced by our desires, fears, and people. Prayer thwarts the temptation to judge programs or people and opens our heart to God's plan.

Activities

In the middle of her second year of ballet, our daughter Cecilia began to complain about *having* to do ballet. Every day at recess her friends practiced their gymnastics skills, and her desire to switch activities increased. Terrell and I prayed and decided that Cecilia needed to complete her program. We seized this opportunity to teach her about making and fulfilling commitments. She was unhappy with our decision but understood the principle. We told her we would continue to pray about the gymnastics because we appreciated her attitude and understood that her interests can change.

Though I loved watching Cecilia dance, God stirred my heart to give fair consideration to gymnastics. I learned that our local recreation center was enrolling children for a four-week gymnastics class. Terrell and I prayed and felt peace to add this to her afternoon schedule, and we hoped that this exposure would show Cecilia and us whether her interest was genuine. Terrell and I delighted to watch her learn quickly and beam with enthusiasm. Additionally, gratitude sparked her attitude to finish ballet strong.

Eight months later, our family moved out of state. A quarter of a mile from our neighborhood was a gymnastics facility. Speechless, we knew: God prepared the way for our little girl. When we moved, she had no friends for a while, and gymnastics gave her something familiar to look forward to every week. Always, God is working a plan—in our heart and in our life.

Relationships

When our children are really young, we have more control over who their playmates are. As they get older, they make these choices, and their peers make choices about them. The friendship journey can be delightfully fun, heartbreaking, and confusing. Pray for your child's relationships and depend on God for discernment. Teach your child to pray for friends and remind her that he gives us our true friends. It's common for a child to have seasons when she doesn't have a friend. Be available for companionship. Lead the child toward friendship with Jesus and pray for this.

Practice: Prayer about Friends

- "God, please bring your friend(s) for each of our children. Lead them to embrace the one(s) that you provide."

- "When it is not your will for there to be a friend, lead me, that I will be who you want me to be in that season. Especially, draw each child toward a deep friendship with you."

- "Lord, I don't know any of these kids. Give me peace with the ones that are your provision. Guard me from judging."

- "Help him make wise choices for friends. Strengthen him to walk away from relationships that are not from you."

As our children get older, opportunities to know their friends can become challenging, but we need to try. Hospitality helps. Become the open home where your children's friends feel welcome. This provides you opportunity to meet and perhaps form relationships with your children's friends. It also enables you to observe what your children are like around their friends.

Time Usage

Occasionally, total the hours for where, with whom, or with what each child spends his time. It may be at school, with a coach, with a friend—or with a computer, the television, or his phone. Sometimes we discover her time is nicely balanced; other times evaluation exposes need for change. Change is hard, especially when a child does not understand the need for a change.

Practice: Steps to Implement Change:

1. Pray daily before the conversation, during the conversation, and throughout the transition, until the child adjusts.

2. Be humble and admit to your child that you have a new point of view.

3. With authority and love, describe what will be different and why. We want the child to understand our decision, though he may not agree with us.

4. Be available to the child as he adjusts. Listen. Observe. Verbally appreciate his effort.

5. Be prepared to meet resistance from the child. Don't react; respond with grace.

6. It's important to remember that, as parents, we can take almost anything away from a child as long as we're willing and ready to replace it with something better—*us*. When we ask, God will show us how to be the replacement that our child really needs.

Throughout life, our child will have times when he is alone or has no plans with others. For a child to see value in alone time, expose him to ways to spend this time. This may challenge you or come naturally, depending on your approach to alone time. Many adults intentionally stay busy or surround themselves with people because they don't want to be alone. Perhaps they were frequently left alone or left alone for inordinately long periods of time without guidance for how to spend their time. Alone and lonely are not meant to be synonymous, but for some people they are.

God wants your child and you to know that you are never alone. As our intimacy with Jesus deepens, we experience this and his peace fills and comforts this space in our heart. When we are present to his nearness, we talk to him more. This would include asking him how to spend alone time or how to walk through an alone season. Later, we look back *changed*. The beauty of God's accomplished purpose in us is a healing balm for the pain and confusion.

Give your child this truth, even if you are learning it with him. Our culture offers countless ways to fill time or be entertained. None can gratify the place in our heart that God created for himself. "Do not be frightened, and do not be dismayed, for the LORD your God is with you wherever you go" (Joshua 1:9b).

God sometimes provides alone time to lead us to discover and develop abilities, pleasures, and traits that he has created in our child. For example, the child experiences his imagination as he designs, builds, and plays; we learn he is creative. We notice that drawing, playing an instrument, reading, or a new hobby brings great pleasure to a child. As we encourage, support, and pray for our child in her new endeavors, traits like self-assurance, perseverance, and contentedness grow.

Unfortunately, we often impulsively fill a child's solitary time with entertainment of some sort. When one form of entertainment inevitably bores the child, her behavior or voice demands a replacement. Electronics are the most common devices used as time fillers or entertainment—Internet exploration, social media, television, movies, videos, and the phone. The devices are not bad—nor is employing them. However, overuse can delay a child's relational development.

Experiences of Success

Success is measured by our child's individual capabilities, progress, attitude, experience, and character development. We want our child to have fun *and* experience personal success.

Regularly evaluate your child's attitude, performance, and self-esteem. Observe, listen, and pray for insight. Humbly review the reason the child is in a particular class or activity. Study the ability of your child and the ability level of other children in the activity. If you discover significant discrepancy, your child may draw an inaccurate negative conclusion about himself. For example, the child may simply need extra help to catch up or build up weak areas. Or, she may benefit to switch to a different instructional level to match her current abilities in order to build a baseline of success. Sometimes, a child's challenging experience is purposed to help her identify her true interests and abilities, as God molds her character. God helps us see.

CONCLUSION

Embrace each season, learn to delegate, take time for yourself, and evaluate your child's and your activities, relationships, and time usage. These practices facilitate our becoming peaceful moms. Peace is available to us daily because God, the source of peace, is with us continually. How we engage with him as we live the day impacts our daily experience of his peace.

Begin. Pray for God's help. He will meet you where you are. It is amazing what he does with a willing heart. God loves his disciples. That's you and me. As we follow, he molds us into the woman of character he already sees—the lovely woman he designed us to be.

Pray. Be near to God. Herein lies our peace.

THINK ABOUT IT

1. Consider simple ways that you can delegate responsibilities in your home.

2. God knows the best time for you to take time for yourself in your current season. Pray to discern when that is and enjoy.

3. Evaluate TV, movies, books, computer games, and video games:

    a. Develop a method of evaluation.

    b. Ask friends to recommend good materials.

    c. Establish time limits.

4. Have you ever considered praying for your child's friendships? How could this be comforting?

5. Does your child have alone time? What benefit do you see?

PART TWO

Become Who You Were
Made to Be

5

A Perspective Makeover

WE MET AS SEVENTH-GRADERS at a party. No sparks flew. In fact,
"hey" was the only word exchanged when mutual friends intro-
duced us. I rejoined my friends and he turned to his. Years passed
and our paths didn't cross. At age twenty-nine, we were surprised
to see one another at the local gym, and a comfortable friendship
evolved. A year later the very unexpected happened—we fell in
love. Before long, Terrell and I were engaged and four months later
happily married. Within two months of marriage I was expecting
our first child. It was a beautiful time in my life.

What makes it fully beautiful is what God did in me in the
first eleven months of that eighteen-month season. That day at the
gym I was in the middle of one of the lowest seasons of my life. I
had great girlfriends, a good job, and a nice friendship with Terrell.
However, I wrestled many days with discouragement. I began to
pray more. I confessed lots of rebelliousness and saw how far I had
distanced myself from God. Tears of self-pity and sadness soaked
my pillow many nights.

Then one night something changed. Lying in the bed, I was
talking to God and unplanned words poured from my mouth:
"God, I feel like a failure. And I want to be married one day, but I
surrender that to you." God moved my heart to know and voice my

deepest feelings. As I whispered it, I knew it to be true; deep inside I did feel like a failure. In the same prayer, he showed me the way forward—surrender to him. I had never surrendered anything to God before.

For several months, I repeated this prayer. I had worked hard to *build* me, to become who I wanted to be or thought I should be. God was changing my perspective—about myself and about him.

When we surrender, we come to realize we are the clay and God is our loving Potter.

God showed the prophet Jeremiah a tangible example of this. He told Jeremiah to walk down to a potter's house and watch as the potter shaped clay. Jeremiah observed:

> And the vessel he was making of clay was spoiled in the potter's hand, and he reworked it into another vessel, as it seemed good to the potter to do. Then the word of the LORD came to me: "... can I not do with you as this potter has done? declares the LORD. Behold, like the clay in the potter's hand, so are you in my hand." (Jeremiah 18:4-6)

Watching a potter work is fascinating. His hands continually work the clay to mold it into the image that he alone envisions. Held in his hands, the clay is his focus as he considers the next step toward his desired outcome.

You and I are God's clay. We are held in his hand. I love this image. Take time to *receive* this blessing—God is *holding* you. He holds your children too. He never puts you down. The verses reveal the intimacy that God the Father desires to have with us. Though we are "spoiled" by sin, he loves us and offers us relationship through Jesus. As we open our heart to Jesus, we become malleable clay. God molds our heart and character like a potter transforms clay. With great love, mercy, tenderness, patience, and power he transforms us to reflect his character.

"Can I not do with you as this potter has done? declares the LORD." A lot of change occurred in those eighteen months—in me and in my life. Each was significant and shaped by God. I lived those days humbled and amazed.

As my due date approached, I remarked to my husband that I did not know how to change a diaper, and he said, "Oh, I do. I'll show you." Rather than assure me, his comment rang my insecurity alarm and ushered in my first tidal wave of feeling completely inadequate. Worry set in. *I don't even know how to change a diaper! What kind of mother will I be?*

Mostly fascinated with the joy of being pregnant and the idea of being a mom, not once did responsibilities of mother-*hood* enter my thoughts. Seeing mothers with their babies and young children made me smile. *I get to do that soon!* I was like the bride who is excited about the wedding but hasn't given much thought to the marriage.

Many of us react anxiously when we lack the knowledge or experience for a parenting circumstance that emerges. If we compare ourself to other moms, we also get discouraged. Through all seasons of motherhood, from infancy through the teen years, most of us fumble through feelings of inadequacy as we face challenges or unfamiliar situations. We have thoughts like:

I don't know what I'm doing!

I don't know how to handle this.

I have no business being a mother.

Maybe I'm not cut out for this. I am a failure at this.

How did things get to this point? Everything is out of control!

At some point each of us face circumstances that overwhelm. We are going to make mistakes. We are going to learn some things the hard way through trial and error. Exhale. This is normal! Inexperience sits on the horizon of every season ahead. Accept this and trust God. He grows and prepares you in the present for the future.

Look in the mirror, and you see an adult. God looks at you and sees your heart. He has vision and hope for you, and he promises to complete his work in you. For all your days on earth, you are his handiwork, in whom he delights and loves deeply.

While we are a work in progress to God, our child is a work in progress to us—though primarily to God. We are *not* our child's potter. What a relief! The Lord molds all of us. In fact, a significant degree of our character molding happens *through* our role as a mother. The Lord intends for mothers and fathers to be his primary vessels in their child's life, to reflect his image in love and character.

God confidently presents a gift to us and issues a call. The gift is our child or children. The call is to be a mother. As his disciples, Jesus wants us to make disciples of our children, partnering with him to raise and shape them to be a godly generation. We are called by God to be missional moms. Our family, our home, is our primary mission field.

GIFT OR BURDEN

Our child is a gift of unconditional love and grace from God; we did not earn him or her. She is part of God's sovereign plan for us, to help us grasp how much he loves us, to help us realize our need for him, and to help us want to grow in him.

Consider how you view your child:

- As a gift, or a burden?
- As someone to love and invest in, or someone to manage and provide for?
- As an instrument of God's love and refining, or a source of stress?

God describes the view we are to have through the psalmist: "Behold, children are a heritage from the LORD, the fruit of the womb a reward" (Psalm 127:3). In the culture, reward is given in response to achievement or merit. God's reward is unmerited favor. My life's history up to now is proof of this. I don't deserve my children, not even one. Many womens' character far exceeds mine. Yet God has given me three children. All is grace. God doesn't evaluate our character and measure our past performance to determine if we deserve to have children. A plan he breathed long ago is in motion. How we respond matters.

Long before God gave you a child, he loved you. Because God first loved us, we are capable of loving our child—not perfectly, but powerfully. If we open our heart to the Lord, he saturates us with love, and this love overflows to our child. Often we don't draw from this limitless reservoir of love. Instead, we operate solely from our feelings.

When our child hurts, disobeys, or disappoints us, we often react and draw from our remaining feelings. Emotion muddles our thoughts, and we liken the child to a burden. *I don't know what to do with her. He is being a pain. She is too much for me to handle.* Do we really want to *do* something with her? Is every aspect of him *a pain*?

Our heart is burdened and our perspective is clouded. The child is not a burden. The burden is the *dynamic* that we cannot fix or control—a particular behavior, an ongoing circumstance, or a dynamic in our relationship.

Feelings register the deep places of our heart, but they are not given to us by God to be our compass. Rather than follow feelings within our heart, God calls us to follow him. He yearns for us to invite him to these deep places. *God, I need you. Please help me.* When we engage with God, he meets us at our weakest place. Watch, listen, be expectant, and ready to follow. God can fan what feels like a flicker of love to a roaring flame.

I remember the first time our infant son cried off and on throughout the night. As the hours passed, every ounce of compassion evaporated, and selfish frustration took over. I finally just sat in the rocking chair in his room, held him, and dozed when he did. All night I fretted and prayed, fretted and prayed. Nothing changed, which frustrated me even more. Not long before the sun would rise, I put him to bed and went to mine.

I woke with the silliest sleep-deprived thought: *I'm waking up in my bed—which means he went to sleep in his. Yay!* Even though I was groggy, I clearly remembered my selfish, grumpy thoughts of last night. As I tiptoed up to his crib, the change in my heart struck me. Just a couple of hours earlier, I was self-consumed by lack of sleep and my inability to soothe our baby. Now, as I looked at him, all I wanted to do was hold him, love him, and spend a new day with him.

Later that morning it dawned on me: *What I felt returning to his room was a glimpse of God's love for me. It is new every morning and unconditional.* His love is not a response to our behavior of yesterday or years before. Then I realized something more. God *did* respond to my prayers that night. While he held my baby and me through the stressful hours, he used that trial *for me* to better comprehend the power of his love.

To be a mother is not a test of endurance or a prison sentence that we're being forced to live out. It is not a means to self-glory whereby we push our child to achieve or become something so that others praise us. Children are gifts from God for us to enjoy, to love and be loved, and to help us draw nearer to him. He honors us to be stewards of another human being—to train, to delight in the fruit of their training, and to lead them to the Lord so that they can know his great love for them.

Be still with God for a few minutes: "Dear God, I receive my child as your gift of love and grace to me. Thank you for _____. Help me receive your love and love my child with your love. Amen."

ANSWER THE CALL

God created the role of mother. First, he created woman to be Adam's helpmate (Genesis 2:18–24). Later he told her that she would bear children (Genesis 3:16). "The man [Adam] called his wife's name Eve, because she was the mother of all living" (Genesis 3:20). After giving birth to her third son, Eve said, "God has appointed for me another child" (Genesis 4.25b, RSV). Eve knew God *gave* her children; she knew God *called her* to be a mother.

Being a mom is a God-appointed role that spans our child's lifetime. How many roles in life have this distinction? Whether we give birth, adopt, or marry someone with children, we are a central part of God's design to reveal his love to each child.

Every believer is called "to live a life worthy of the calling you have received" (Ephesians 4:1b, NIV). Paul writes specifically about the primary call to live a worthy life as a follower of Christ. Yet his words can apply to each particular calling we receive from God as his followers. One such calling is motherhood.

We are challenged to live a *worthy* life as mothers. Worthy does not mean perfect. Only God is perfect. A worthy life is one that honors God and reflects commitment to him. The more we love him, the more we want to live for him—to follow and obey him. God honors us with the opportunity and privilege to participate with him in molding our child, as he molds us.

There is no substitute for a mother. Know that you are very important to the life of your child. Receive the call. If you have never considered motherhood as a calling, take this minute to pray: "God, I accept your call. Thank you for this blessing and for your confidence in me. Help me to follow you and live a worthy life. Amen."

SIGNIFICANCE AS A WOMAN

I hope I see someone to talk to. Climbing the stairs to the wedding reception, I felt grateful for all fifteen steps. I discreetly exhaled, attempting to rid anxiety from my pounding heart. *Where is this coming from?* Then I knew. *I am alone; usually I'm with Terrell or joined at the hip or hand with a child.* Driving home later that night, I prayed, *God, I don't ever want to feel like that again. This is another layer, isn't it? You're uncovering another vulnerable place in my heart.*

God frequently uses circumstances to expose places in our heart that he wants to heal, make whole, and set free. The process can be humbling, even painful at times. For example, I was humbled when I realized that my security was wrapped up in my family. The anxiety I struggled through that night was hard, but the pain got my attention. God wanted to help me, and I needed help.

The root of anxiety is fear. Fear fueled my experience of insecurity and anxiety. Fear grips many of us—fear of what others think, fear of rejection, fear of displeasing, fear of all the worst possibilities, fear of failing. We can identify our fear and go to God for healing and freedom. "There is no fear in love, but perfect love casts out fear" (1 John 4:18a).

Perfect Love casts out fear. God is Perfect Love. God casts out fear. He exposes it—and waits for us to invite and receive Perfect Love. Once we truly believe in our heart that he loves us, we turn to him as our source for significance.

"What a person desires is unfailing love . . ." (Proverbs 19:22a, NIV). We need to know we are loved—to feel and experience it. Other yearnings manifest from this desire—to feel valued and accepted. God creates us with this desire because he wants to fulfill it through our commitment to a covenant relationship with him. He is Unfailing Love.

Are you familiar with trials of feeling insecure or unworthy? Are you ready for those to end?

Jesus says, "Behold, I stand at the door and knock. If anyone hears my voice and opens the door, I will come in to him and eat with him, and he with me" (Revelation 3:20). Jesus comes to us, but we have to open the door. Our heart is the door. Once we open the door, Jesus enters, dwells, and relationship begins. Open wide the door to your heart. Receive the fullness of his love poured out for you—and to you.

God gave Jesus to humankind to die for our sins, and he raised him from the dead for our salvation and his glory. "For God so loved the world, that he gave his only Son, that whoever believes in him should not perish but have eternal life. For God did not send his Son into the world to condemn the world, but in order that the world might be saved through him" (John 3:16–17). This relationship is our first step toward freedom.

Since I was a little girl, I believed that Jesus loves me and died for my sins. I prayed to him for help and for things I wanted, and I thanked him when he answered my prayers. I told him I loved him a lot. I cried to him when I was hurt.

At age thirty-two, I first heard the term "personal relationship with Jesus." I did not know there was a more intimate experience of his love to be pursued and received. I did not know that Jesus wants to talk to me and be intimately involved in the day-to-day of my life, simply because I mean that much to him. For years, I pursued people and accomplishment for such significance. *I did not know there was more.* You might not either. The most authentic understanding of being loved and giving love comes through having a personal relationship with Jesus Christ.

That night I told Jesus that I wanted to have a personal relationship with him. Over the next few months, I realized that the stress of measuring up or worrying about what others think still rattled me. Because we tend to understand love and worth by the way people have or haven't loved us, we struggle to believe God's love is sufficient. For the record, the two are incomparable! To believe God's love is a step of *faith* in God. I prayed that he would establish me in his love. Through the exercises below I grew to realize God's love is truly unconditional and completely sufficient. His love became my anchor.

Practice: Experience God's Love

1. Surrender to God every person, activity, and relationship through which you seek value or affirmation. With each release, invite God to fill this place: "Dear God, fill this void in my heart with your love. Amen."

2. Read what God says about his love. Do a word study of "love." Use the concordance in the back of your Bible. A study Bible has more references. You learn about God's love for his people, which includes you. Before each passage pray: "God, as I read, help me receive your love for me. Establish your love in my heart. Please continue to expose who and what else I depend on in place of you. Amen."

We shortchange ourself when we measure our significance through our achievements, relationships, or occupation. When we seek the approval of others or fear their rejection, we choose people's opinion toward us instead of God's truth. God has so much to say to you. Listen, be loved, and learn. Seek and savor his perspective of you.

Make this passage from Ephesians a daily prayer for your children and yourself by substituting your children's names and your name for "you."

> For this reason I bow my knees before the Father, from whom every family in heaven and on earth is named, that according to the riches of his glory he may grant you to be strengthened with power through his Spirit in your inner being, so that Christ may dwell in your hearts through faith—that you, being rooted and grounded in love, may have strength to comprehend with all the saints what is the breadth and length and height and depth, and to know the love of Christ that surpasses knowledge, that you may be filled with all the fullness of God. (Ephesians 3:14–19)

SIGNIFICANCE AS A MOM

Many of us experience honor through an accomplishment or a title. For example, in school we made the honor roll, got elected to a student government office, or earned accolades in athletics or the arts. As we serve in our community or work professionally, praise or recognition is common. We are conditioned to be productive and to perform in order to feel significant or deserving of honor.

Personal achievement or words of recognition gratify temporarily a yearning in our heart for significance. Understandably, as we become mothers, we anticipate similar feelings of gratification, based on our experiences in other endeavors. In the quiet of our heart we hope for that same sense of fulfillment and significance. We make considerable effort to be good moms, but many days we feel defeated, discouraged, and unproductive.

"I felt better about myself before I became a mother. I was confident in my job."

"I never seem to be able to finish any thing I start."

"No one appreciates what I do. Half the time, I don't see anything significant about what I do."

"I don't feel like I'm making any headway with my kids."

We're grateful for our children and love them deeply, but our inner struggle is painful. At home, appreciation is expressed when we require good manners, and the closest thing to constructive feedback is talkback. The experience of accomplishment is measured on the tiniest of scales—the laundry got folded, no one complained about supper, everyone is in bed on time. In the ordinary day of being a mom, it is challenging to feel significant or to believe we are accomplishing anything of significance.

We look to the left and right and see what other moms do. Even if we do similar things, we compare. We measure our output and sense of accomplishment, and then we judge ourself. One week we feel good about ourself, but a month later a new circumstance shakes our self-perspective.

Conflicting feelings wear us down. In one breath we admire an active mom friend: *She is so creative and shares her abilities with so many.* But as we exhale, we compare ourself to her: *How does she balance it all?* That mom we admire does what we wish we could or think we should do. We attempt to solve or resolve who we think we need to be right now in life, as a mom, in order to feel significant.

"Are not two sparrows sold for a penny? And not one of them will fall to the ground apart from your Father. But even the hairs of your head are all numbered. Fear not, therefore; you are of more value than many sparrows" (Matthew 10:29–31). Jesus describes God's attentiveness and how uniquely we are made. He responds to our worry—"Fear not." In other words, stop worrying because his value for us is great and sufficient.

Quite a few women in the Scriptures are identified as someone's mother. Their names are not followed by a list of activities to substantiate their significance. When God appoints mothers (and fathers), he calls us to a tremendous responsibility. He *bestows* honor on you.

His esteem for the significance of this is role is displayed in the fifth of his Ten Commandments. "Honor your father and your mother, that your days may be long in the land that the LORD your God is giving you" (Exodus 20:12). This commandment is repeated in five other places: Deuteronomy 5:16; Matthew 15:4 and 19:19; Mark 7:10; and Ephesians 6:2. God commands all who love him to honor their mother and father.

Have you considered the magnitude of the responsibility and honor God gives you?

Rather than chase significance, pursue God. He knows who you can be as you live loved and live a worthy life. Receive his honor. Peace comes when our perspective changes. Significance as a mom blossoms in our heart when we believe God's love, believe he gave us this role, and believe his already-designed plan for us will glorify him. He satisfies our yearnings with his peace and unfolds his way to live each day.

Being a mom is not glamorous or about recognition.

Being a mom is about *humility*: We make mistakes and live on a learning curve.

Being a mom is about *selflessness*: We put our child's needs before our own because he depends on us and we're responsible for him.

Being a mom is about *sacrifice*: For a season we give up things we enjoyed before we had children. We decline some opportunities because we're first committed to raising our children.

Being a mom is about *grace*: We recognize our weaknesses and need God's grace to be who God knows we can be.

Being a mom is about *quiet reward*: When we see our child grow in the Lord; when we see him respond to our love and discipleship; when we see her become the person of character that God made her to be.

Being a mom is about *blessing beyond what this world sees as valuable*: When we know the wonderful and tangible love of our child and that immeasurable inner peace that we are partnering with God, who gave us this gift and honor.

THINK ABOUT IT

1. Isn't it comforting to know that we are a work in progress—being molded like clay in the Potter's hands, rather than being expected to get everything right by a certain age?

   a. How can we apply this concept as we raise our child?

2. What challenges you to believe that your role as a mom is very significant?

   a. My self esteem before I had children.

   b. I compare this to the lifestyle I had before I had children.

   c. What I see other mothers do outside the home.

   d. Describe other challenges.

3. From where, whom, or what do you tend to get your worth or security?

4. Does God's love fill your places of insecurity, or do you think people and responsibilities fill those places in your heart?

   a. If you do not have a personal relationship with Jesus, consider praying for this now.

   b. If you do, pray for someone who does not.

5. Have you ever considered the magnitude of the responsibility and honor that God gives *you*?

   a. Pray and receive his honor.

6

Relationship

THE MORE WE VALUE a person, the more we pursue relationship. We want to know her, and we hope she's interested to know us. We set apart time to get to know each other. We talk to share about ourself, and we listen in order to know her better.

Cultivating a relationship with God is similar. We set apart time to get to know him, talk to him, and listen to him. God knows us thoroughly and through his Word he makes himself known to us. He doesn't make having a relationship hard or complicated. We do.

His foremost call to us is to be followers of Christ, through pursuing relationship with him. When this relationship is not our first priority, someone or something else is. None of us want to admit this might be true. Our thoughts and behavior say it for us.

God sees who or what receives our primary focus, and he knows the insufficiency we will eventually experience. Even still, he holds us in the palm of his mighty hand and loves us. Because he abounds in grace, he waits for us to turn around and love him as our Everything.

GET TO KNOW HIM

"Have you ever had a quiet time?" my husband of a month asked.

"A what?"

"A quiet time. I think you would like it." He proceeded to describe it.

"Sounds nice . . . I'll have to try that *one day.*"

At the time, the pace of the learning curve unfolding in my life overwhelmed me. I was a newlywed, newly pregnant, and trying to figure out the role of a minister's wife while also learning what my minister-husband does. I was adjusting to a new denomination, a new church, meeting lots of new faces, and teaching full-time. The truth was, I did not *want* to learn or try to fit *one more new thing* into my life.

Where will I insert this into my day? No obvious answer to this question was my first excuse to put it off. The fact that I didn't own a Bible was my second excuse. My experience with Scripture was what I heard in church and school. My third excuse exposed my heart. I was intimidated to study Scripture. I worried that I wouldn't understand what I read, much less get a deeper message from the verses. I presumed that reading Scripture was easy for everyone *else.*

A couple of months passed. My learning curve was still large, yet this idea of a quiet time kept returning to my thoughts, partly as a "should do" and partly because I was curious about this thing my husband really valued.

Define quiet time? I can tell you what I do, but everyone structures his or hers differently. By the way, you don't have to call it that. Call it whatever you like. My quiet time is alone time with God to be still, quietly present and available to him. I read the Scriptures and journal what stirs my heart and mind. For example, a verse might challenge, comfort, or provide guidance. I may paraphrase a passage to better understand it. Sometimes my words express an intimate response from my heart to what I think God is saying to me through his Word. Next, I pray. I try to still my thoughts to listen for his. Thanks, praise, admitting disobedience, asking for help or healing, and unloading burdens can all be a part of this. I divide intercession for loved ones into different days of the week. One day I decided it was time to face my apprehension. I asked Terrell to buy me a Bible. He probably had to pinch himself to keep his jaw from dropping open. Wise man—he hid any reaction from me. The next day he came home with a study Bible, including side tabs that mark where each book begins within the Bible. A few days later, on the way home from work, I decided to give it a try. I held the Bible sideways to identify the thinner books. I wanted to experience success, to know that I could understand and finish one book in this Book. I chose the book of Ruth because it was my grandmother's name. And I opened my new spiral notebook in case I wanted to jot thoughts.

If I sound like a child . . . I *felt* like a child. Looking back, it probably was a beginning place for me to understand I *am* a child, in grown-up skin, loved by an amazing Father.

Lord, I feel so intimidated. Help me do this. After reading a few verses, I paraphrased what I read in my notebook. Then I added a few life application thoughts that the verses stirred in me. In all, this took about twenty minutes. Instead of feeling alone, I felt like I was stepping in to a privileged intimacy with God.

I smile when I recall what a mountain I made of attempting this. Instead, it was a quiet, simple, easy experience. Truly, it is one of the most significant days of my life. I added a dimension to my relationship with God and to my quality of life.

Does my initial struggle strike a chord in your heart?

One day I was talking with a mother of three young children about quiet time. She sighed, "I can't wait to start having a quiet time." When I asked why she was waiting, she answered, "Well, I'm waiting for my youngest to begin preschool. Then I'll have some time for myself."

God wants us to get to know him *now*. He created us for *this* relationship. That means there is time in your day, in your current season. Be encouraged. We have to *want* to spend time with God—not in an obligated sense, but with heartfelt desire. When we do, we will ask him to show us the *when*. Identifying this time to set apart with the Lord is our individual and humble journey toward realizing the time was always there. We were just doing something else with it.

"All scripture is breathed out by God and profitable for teaching, for reproof, for correction, and for training in righteousness, that the man of God may be complete, equipped for every good work" (2 Timothy 3:16–17). God gave us the Bible to learn about him, to learn to discern his voice, and to be equipped for living—which includes being a mom.

After my first quiet time, I struggled to make time for this. Responsibilities, tasks, and giving in to tiredness won precedence. I grew frustrated with my inconsistency. *How am I consistent with so many other things—but this? If I have time to exercise, talk on the phone, check email, and look through catalogs, certainly I can find ten minutes to spend alone with God in his Word.*

Then I got it. My quiet time was not a priority. It was just another thing "to do."

I decided that a daily appointment with God is a priority for me. *God, show me the best time of day to have my quiet time with you.* He did. Of course, something else had to go. For me, it was a little morning sleep. I silently whined at first. Actually, I whined plenty of mornings as I crawled out of bed having been up several times with the children during the night. But what got me up each morning was the memory of each experience of the days before. It was always worth it. Though I was physically exhausted many mornings, I received God's spiritual rest and restoration. The rest he gives is far more sustaining than the surrendered thirty minutes of sleep!

Some days I think, "Wow, that's just what I needed to read today," or "These verses really challenge me—in a good way." Other times I don't feel particularly inspired or even understand what I have read. And that's okay. Every time we choose to be still with God in his Word, we demonstrate our commitment to this relationship. Our effort says, "God, I love you and I want to know you. You are my first priority." When we show up, God responds.

We may not sense it at the time, but he is present and works in our heart in ways that one day we will see.

What an awesome privilege—sitting alone with Almighty God. Spending time in the Scriptures nourishes our soul. God feeds us with sustaining Truth. Like manna was for the Israelites, his nourishment is available to us every day. We have to choose to pick it up and be fed.

Just like we nurture our children, God wants to nurture us through our relationship and through his Word. Reflect on these questions:

- To whom or what do I turn for nourishment and restoration?
- Do I make effort to spend time with God like I make effort to spend time with others I love?

Lovingly, God waits for us to decide to give him some of the time he has given us. We're the ones missing out.

When we read the Bible, far more happens that learning facts about God and history. We get to know him and his character, and he gives insight about ours. As we welcome him to affect our heart, he reveals unhealed wounds and heals us; he convinces us to forgive and seek forgiveness; he shows our strengths and how to apply them; he shows our weaknesses and how to overcome them.

We are changed through the power of God's Word working in our life. How we speak, how we love, how we forgive, and how we discipline are influenced. Our children benefit as we learn to love and relate through God's inspiration. We can pass on to our children the truths of God that we experience and spiritual disciplines that we have embraced.

Practice: Steps for a Quiet Time

1. Purchase a devotional or select a book in Scripture that intrigues you.
2. Determine a time in your day. Ask God what time is best for you.

3. Start with ten minutes.

4. Aim to do this two to three days in the week. Pray for God's strength to persevere. Ask a friend to pray for you to establish this time.

5. Once you're in a rhythm of three days a week, try to add a fourth day and so on.

6. As you can, add more time to each day.

7. Be flexible. Some days or seasons may require us to "reschedule our appointment."

My husband once told me that my having a quiet time is the most important gift that I give to him and to our children every day. He is comforted that I go to God as my Source for love, direction, answers, and everything else that I need. He's encouraged to know that if anyone in our family has a problem—including us—I will go to God for direction.

"Satisfy us in the morning with your steadfast love, that we may rejoice and be glad all our days" (Psalm 90:14). God satisfies our needs with his love. Fed by his Word and established in his love, we have the capacity to love others in the fullest way.

TALK

Sometimes in desperation, other times in joy, but mostly to retain (or regain) focus, I pray. God wants us to come to him about everything. The more you talk to him the more you will experience this to be true. Praying reminds me I am never alone. The Lord is my primary confidante, the one I talk to most in a day.

"I don't want to bother God with this. Lots of people have bigger problems."

"He's probably tired of me coming to him about this."

Our needs, desires, and prayers are not measured or compared by God. He is not partial. He wants us to trust him as *all*—in all. God is with us always, but many hours of the day we don't act like he is. We take care of ourself, or we depend on and vent to other people. We miss much when we don't go to God. He wants us to engage with him like a constant companion. This means our flow of thought and emotion is said to him. As we engage, we grow aware of his guidance, nearness, and response.

Sure, God already knows our thoughts and can see our heart, but he wants an intimate relationship. He wants us to experience sharing with him and learning to discern his response. He invites us to trust him and witness his faithfulness. Jesus encourages us, "Ask, and it will be given to you; seek, and you will find; knock, and it will be opened to you. For every one who asks receives, and the one who seeks finds, and to the one who knocks it will be opened" (Matthew 7:7-8). Jesus promises he will respond. We ask and seek, yet we grow to *desire* what he knows is best.

Practice: Ways to Talk to God

- Share frustration. God wants us to be real with him: "Lord, I'm so frustrated with their bickering that I could scream! I give you my anger. Please give me your grace."
- Acknowledge his work. Celebrate his goodness: "Thank you for a parking place right by the building. You are so good to me."
- Ask for comfort: "Lord, I'm afraid of the path she is heading down."
- Ask for wisdom: "Please tell me or show me why my child is has withdrawn."

LISTEN

During our first year of marriage, I periodically found myself in the company of a group of women in our church who intrigued me. They talked about the Lord as though he really was their constant companion.

"I wonder if the Lord is saying . . ."

"I think the God might be leading me to . . ."

"I was praying yesterday and this picture came to my mind. I wonder if it's from the Lord . . ."

"This verse continues to come to mind . . ."

"I asked God how . . ."

"He gave me the words to say . . ."

My parents faithfully taught the importance of prayer, but it was a private experience, except at meals and in church. To listen to God was a new concept for me. The fact that I could learn to sense God communicating with me fascinated me. *I want to be able to do that—to hear God.* I began to pray earnestly, "Lord, I want to learn to hear your voice." Soon I added, "How will I know it's your voice? Help me learn to discern your voice from my thoughts. Help me know when I have heard you just one time!"

Have you ever said, "That sounds like something he would say"? You're familiar with that person's character. The more we know God and his character, the more he sharpens our discernment of his voice. He wants us to hear him. In the Bible, we are exhorted to hear and listen to him. Reading Scripture is a tremendously helpful exercise because it is God's words written. He inspired the authors who penned the words so that we might know him more fully.

When someone suggested I could learn to hear God through reading Scripture, I wondered if God would only speak to me with Bible verses. Honestly, I thought this would be a funny way to answer some of my questions! *What should I fix for supper? Who should we invite to the party?* God certainly speaks or answers us through Scripture, but it is not the only way.

"Hearing" God's voice translates to a different experience for each of us. Some have individual words, phrases, or sentences come to mind, while others see images or pictures in their thoughts. You may receive a sense in your heart that God is leading you in a particular direction. To discern God's meaning, ask him for understanding. He often provides additional circumstances that seem to confirm what we think God is communicating. We are his sheep and he is our Shepherd. He draws us near so that we hear him. "The sheep hear his voice, and he calls his own sheep by name and leads them out. When he has brought out all his own, he goes before them, and the sheep follow him, for they know his voice" (John 10:3b–4).

Praise, spoken or sung, is a wonderful way to intentionally turn our focus to God, so that other thoughts and circumstances of the day fall away. The Psalms provide good examples of praise, as do hymns and contemporary worship music. When we worship God with praise, we posture our heart toward him. Our mind clears to hear his whisper.

Another way to practice listening for God's voice is to pray with our spouse, a friend, or a small group. When my children took naps, a friend and I met weekly at my home to pray for our families and practice listening. Later I joined a group that met to pray for our church. In both settings we began with praise, agreed to be quiet to listen, and only prayed aloud what we humbly *thought* might be something God's was stirring in us. Sometimes an image, verse, or thought would remain with me, so I'd share it with the group. The others did the same. Often what we shared was confirmed through another person present. It was a sweet time to quietly worship and be encouraged as we sought to hear God.

Be patient. Discerning God's voice is a lifelong process. Being still in his presence, his peace floods our soul.

CONCLUSION

Raising our children in a culture with unstable and inconsistent morals is exhausting. Gathering with Christian moms to share, learn, and minister to one another can be beneficial. However, being a Christian does not mean we all have the same opinions about standards for what is appropriate and inappropriate. "Do not be conformed to this world, but be transformed by the renewal of your mind, that by testing you may discern what is the will of God, what is good and acceptable and perfect" (Romans 12:2).

God calls us to relationship with him, that we can know him and follow him. Our personal relationship with Jesus is the most important thing in our life. As we study his Word, pray, and listen, we learn that our calling as a mother is not a solo feat. It is an opportunity to partner intimately with the One who gave us this role.

THINK ABOUT IT

1. Have you ever accepted the truth that God wants you to get to know him?

   a. How could this contribute to being a peaceful mom?

2. If you regularly spend time in the Scriptures, that is great. If this is a new or uncomfortable topic for you, I know how you feel. Unload to God obstacles that hinder you from spending time in his Word, and invite him to show you his way forward.

   a. Ask other friends how they fit this time into their week.

3. God loves us more than we can imagine. How often do you think he would like us to talk to him throughout the day?

   a. At the beginning and end of the day. How we get through the rest of the day is up to us.

   b. One lengthy time a day. He knows we are busy making our day happen.

   c. Throughout the day. He wants to participate with us all day long, leading and encouraging us throughout.

PART THREE

Navigating the Bumpy Road of Commitments

7

Overcommitted, Uncommitted, or Somewhere in Between

"WHERE DID THIS DAY GO?"

As the day begins, we anticipate sufficient time to get things done. Then we look at the clock and it is time to fix supper.

Being a mom, we are naturally busy. We drive carpool, change diapers, do laundry, help with homework after we figure out *how* to do the homework, home school, settle squabbles, put band-aids on skinned knees, put hugs on wounded hearts, clean the house, grocery shop, and then turn those groceries into a meal. Whew! And that's just on the home front.

We are committed to our children. If we weren't, we would probably run away!

For many of us, caring for our children is not our only responsibility or commitment. If we are married, we make commitments to our husband and to grow our marriage. If we are employed, we commit to perform specific duties. We make commitments to volunteer in our community, including involvement in our church. We try to nurture extended family relationships and friendships.

Are you tired yet? No wonder the days seem to evaporate.

Some seasons we are content with the pace and components of our life because the rhythm seems manageable, fulfilling, even peaceful. Then in a blink, it seems, we struggle to account for how busy life has become.

Busyness does not happen all of a sudden. Busyness is built—one circumstance, decision, or incidental at a time. A new circumstance within the family—a job change, a new school, a health issue, a relational matter, or a move—affects us emotionally, alters the daily rhythm, and may disrupt familiar schedules. A decision to add a commitment, small or large, brings more responsibility and collects more of our time. Incidentals are a given. These unexpected errands, school assignments, doctor appointments, and conversations frequently absorb time that we already considered taken.

Our approach to making commitments is varied. We overcommit, hesitate to commit, commit for the wrong reason, or avoid commitment. Read the following charts to identify your familiar patterns. Most of us exercise more than one. Think about and talk with God about how each of your patterns influences you. Does is contribute to a peaceful rhythm for you? Does it frustrate or burden you?

Reasons We Make Commitments:

1. For love: We marry, have children, develop relationships with extended family, and cultivate friendships.

2. Passion: We realize God has equipped us with gifts and given us passion to exercise them.

3. We see need and want to meet it.

4. We can't say no.

5. We want to contribute to feel significant.

6. We want to meet people, or we may be lonely.

7. We need or want more money.

8. We want to fill a void in our life.

9. It sounds fun.

Reasons We Don't Make Commitments:

1. We have issues with fear:

   Fear of failing—*What if I can't do it? What if I mess up?*

   Fear of inadequacy—*I'm sure someone else can do a better job than me. What do I have to contribute?*

   Fear of people—We may not know how to comfortably engage with others.

2. We are uncomfortable to contact someone we do not know.

   We struggle to believe a person or group would want us to join them.

   We are shy.

3. We grew up in a home where no one made or kept commitments—to the family or to others. This is our learned behavior.

4. We are lazy. Motivation is inspired by benefit to self.

Commitment opportunities emerge throughout life. Each provides practice for us to pause, pray, and invite God to navigate. Our approach to making commitments is a response. We respond to God, to ourself, or to someone else. When we respond to ourself or someone else, gratification may come initially, but often frustration or emptiness follows. When we respond to God, satisfaction and his peace fill us.

He hopes that we will serve him with the gifts and abilities he created in us—yet follow his guidance to know when. He encourages our strengths and strengthens our weaknesses. He knows where we need healing and where we will benefit to be humbled. He leads us to step *in* to a commitment and alerts us to step *back* from one.

God wants to help, heal, and lead us to live healthier lives. Pray. Each time we welcome him in to another area of our life, we open the door to more freedom and peace.

Practice: Making Commitments

1. Invite God: "Please reveal unhealthy reasons that I make or avoid commitments." Specific experiences might come to mind that help you identify this.

2. Name and release the reason(s): "Lord, I see that I _____. I release that to you."

3. Invite God to have this emptied place in your heart: "I invite you to have this place in my heart. Please fill me with your love and heal me."

4. Ask for strength and help: "Strengthen me to apply what you have shown me. Teach me healthy patterns."

A FRESH APPROACH

Changing our ways is not easy. Willingness to change our approach for making commitments is a giant step forward. You will see the positive effect on your disposition and your children and be encouraged.

"Commit your way to the LORD; trust in him, and he will act" (Psalm 37:5). Apply this verse for your day or as you consider a commitment. *God, I commit my way to you. I trust you and believe that you will act.* When we yield our plan, we decide to trust God and his plan. He knows the plan we had and how hard it is to let it go. He sustains our heart.

God knows what your family can handle, and he knows what you can manage *with his help*. Pause to evaluate your current commitments and theirs before forging ahead to add another one. Consider the emotional and physical impact of a new circumstance or decision.

God faithfully guides. Sometimes it's hard to discern his guidance when we lean emotionally in a particular direction. Often a sense of inner peace confirms when we accurately sense his leading. When God's answer isn't the answer we *want*, honestly express this to him. He is our comforter and blankets our heart with his love. We learn in time that God always gives us his best.

TRUST GOD

This verse soothes and redirects my heart when I wrestle through making a decision:

> Trust in the LORD with all your heart, and do not rely on your own insight. In all your ways acknowledge him, and he will make straight your paths. Do not be wise in your own eyes; fear the LORD, and turn away from evil. It will be healing for your flesh and a refreshment for your bones. (Proverbs 3:5–8, RSV)

Sometimes we pray and we still aren't sure what to do, especially when it comes to commitments. An opportunity turns our head, or our child's head, because it matches our interests, strengths, or needs.

When our children were young, we wanted to expose them to a variety of activities. I prayed about my decisions regarding them. However, when I talked with other moms and heard all that their children were doing, I sometimes second-guessed my decisions. One day this thought came to mind: *God made my children. He created in each of them particular interests and abilities. He wants to help us know good times for each of them to do certain things—and when not to do other things. God is the one who enables my children to thrive.* This perspective brought great peace to my heart.

"For everything there is a season, and a time for every matter under heaven" (Ecclesiastes 3:1). All of our life is not right now. All of our child's life is not right now.

THE CHILD'S COMMITMENTS

God sees the true condition of our family and each member. He knows what each person needs *now*, what could strain or strengthen particular relationships, and what the family schedule can handle at this time and in the near future. Our role is to partner with him. We follow his lead, and our child follows ours. As we practice making our commitments by partnering with God, it gets easier to teach our child. Our personal examples will flow authentically as we encourage him.

When our children were little, I began to pray about their activities. If I had peace, I asked the child about participating in the activity, to which he always said yes. When a child initiated the conversation about an activity, we agreed that we would pray together *and* individually for several days. Then we talked about our prayer times.

Our child needs to learn to go to Jesus for guidance about his life. A good place to begin is teaching him to pray about commitments. As the child talks to him about which activities to join, continue, or discontinue, he adds a new dimension to his personal relationship with Jesus. At first, more of his experience may be at the level of having peace—or not—about an activity.

For example, if your seven-year-old son mentions joining the basketball league in the fall, respond gently, "That could be great. We can start praying about that every day to see what God says. He knows what will be the most fun for you right now. And, whenever you think about basketball, just say a quick prayer." Of course, pray for the child to pray. He is learning a new skill.

If praying out loud with your child is unfamiliar, God knows and helps. After all, we are talking to him. Practice by casually praying aloud about simple things. *Jesus, help her with her test. Please heal his cold.* As a child hears and participates in prayer more frequently, it becomes familiar. Soon it won't seem unusual to pray about commitments.

As a child gets older, he is less likely to want to pray with us. Consider this a transition time in his walk with God—not an end. Casually, provide direction that includes encouragement.

Practice: Conversation to Point an Older Child toward Prayer

Child: "I'm thinking about trying out for the tennis team."

Mom: "Great, thanks for telling me. I will pray for you to know God's leading."

Child: [No words, just a nod]

Mom: [Another day] "Any new thoughts about basketball when you pray?"

Child: "I haven't prayed."

Mom: "Oh, Okay. Just keep in mind God wants you to have his best. He is committed to you. He wants you to ask him because he wants relationship with you. He will lead you."

Child: "Okay."

Mom: "Whenever you think about tennis, just pray and ask him. It's that easy."

"I will instruct you and teach you in the way you should go; I will counsel you with my eye upon you" (Psalm 32:8). We experience God's faithfulness to these words over and over again. Assure your child of God's faithful counsel. This is discipleship. We instruct and show our child the blessing of relationship with Jesus *and* how to relate with him in the ordinary day. Don't wait for a big smile or a thank-you. Precede and follow every effort with prayer. Pray that the child will pray. Pray for deepening intimacy in his relationship with Jesus. Pray for protection and strengthening in your relationship with your child. Quietly and humbly enjoy the privilege of sharing Jesus and making a disciple. We sow seeds and water with prayer. God gives growth.

When we don't pray to determine whether or not do an activity, this does not mean that we miss out on God's blessing. That sounds like conditional love. God blesses and loves his children with everlasting love. Selecting the right activities isn't the main thing. The main thing is cultivating a relationship with Jesus.

To genuinely ask him for direction takes faith—a willingness to trust that he will respond and that his guidance will work out for our best. When we learn to ask, he meets us and helps us take the next big step—to follow his way. Trust deepens such that we want to follow his plan more and more. As our trust in the Lord grows, we want our child to have the same rich relationship that we enjoy with him. All along way, God's peace reigns in our heart and in our home.

THINK ABOUT IT

1. To what commitment do you give the most time in a week? Examples: marriage, children, work, volunteer activity, hobby, Internet, housework, exercise.

2. How do your commitments, or lack of them, affect your parenting?

3. Have you ever considered inviting God into your commitment-making decisions? How could this benefit you as a woman and as a mom?

4. Name advantages for praying about each child's commitments.

5. If you were to lead your child to pray about her commitments:
   a. How could this affect her choices?

   b. Do you think it could build the bond between you? How?

8

The Example to Follow

I CANNOT THINK OF a year, while raising our children, that I did not hit the wall of overwhelm. Typically, it happened at random times—picking up toys as the children napped, in the car while running errands, settling a squabble between kids, or watching a child walk through an ongoing painful situation. The words would fall out of my mouth: "I am overwhelmed." My first utterance always felt like I was throwing up the white flag—not in a humble, yielded way, but more like: *I've had it. I give up.* Then I would sit down and stare into space for a while. *I can't give up, so what do I do now?* I wish I could say that I immediately started praying, but I didn't. However, each time I said this was actually progress for me. It meant that I had hit my limit for what I could handle and that something had to change. When I was ready to admit that *my way* wasn't working, then my words-to-self became words-to-God.

I don't recall hints or signals that momentum was building— so that I might realize that I was heading toward overwhelm. I am sure this is because from the beginning of any day to the end, I just keep moving. Sure, I sit—for a meeting or to ride in the car—but not to intentionally rest.

We are human and we misstep—even if we pray and plan. Usually, we misstep several times before it dawns on us that perhaps something needs to *change*. We tend to repeat our patterns until we ask God to change our heart and help us. So, one day I humbly raised another white flag. *God, I don't want to do things my way any more. Please change my heart and help me follow you.*

> Listen carefully: Unless a grain of wheat is buried in the ground, dead to the world, it is never any more than a grain of wheat. But if it is buried, it sprouts and reproduces itself many times over. In the same way, anyone who holds on to life just as it is destroys that life. But if you let it go, reckless in your love, you'll have it forever, real and eternal. If any of you wants to serve me, then follow me. Then you'll be where I am, ready to serve at a moment's notice. The Father will honor and reward anyone who serves me. Right now I am storm-tossed. And what am I going to say? "Father, get me out of this"? No, this is why I came in the first place. I'll say, "Father, put your glory on display." (John 12:24–28, MSG)

Nearing his time on the cross, Jesus tells a story to warn and exhort his followers for how to live day to day. He sees their daily challenge: Live as the culture does or trust him and lay down their ways for his.

Jesus describes a living grain of wheat. Can you picture it, blowing in the wind in a field? If it remains there, the grain will not fulfill its intended purpose. To be fruitful it must die, lose its life. Dead, it becomes seed. The seed is new life, and it will sprout and reproduce many times over.

Jesus likens the grain of wheat to us. Like the grain blowing in the wind, we live and actively move about. *But where are we going and what is our intended purpose?* If we desire clarity of purpose and a truly fruitful life, Jesus warns that we have to "let it go."

Are you ready to surrender your life?

We may not realize how we hold our life—and perhaps our child's—in our clenched fist. We do what we want to do, and our way seems to work. However, Jesus warns that if we live as we please, which is the way of the culture, then we will lose the blessed and purposeful life that God intends.

We cannot live both ways. Our willful pattern has to die so God's way can sprout in us. In order for our old life to die, we repent or turn from old patterns and relinquish control of how we approach life. We stop scheduling to suit ourself or someone else. We stop avoiding what we don't *want*. We entrust our living to Christ. Our clenched fist becomes an open hand that can slide into the perfect hand of God.

Practice: Prayer of Release

Open your hands and pray: "Dear God, I have held my life and my child's life tightly in my hand. I release to you the way I make decisions about commitments (describe) and the way I approach living my life (describe) and the way I make decisions about my child's commitments (describe). I choose to *let it go*. I surrender the way I live, to you. I choose to trust you. Empower and lead me. Amen."

Themes in Jesus' life make for interesting parallels for moms: When he taught and trained his disciples, he seized teachable moments and creatively tried to get his point across. People often wanted something from him. He spent a lot of time listening, comforting, and praying for those he loved. He invested time to build relationships and to point people to God. His life was full. He served the people. All the while, Jesus endured rejection, ridicule, and meanness.

Do some of these themes of Jesus' life have a ring of familiarity? Of course, his challenges tremendously exceed ours. However, the Gospel accounts of Matthew, Mark, Luke, and John let us glean much from the way Jesus lived *through* his challenges. His approach provides the example we can follow for how to live and shape each day.

STAY ALERT

"For we do not have a high priest who is unable to sympathize with our weaknesses, but one who in every respect has been tempted as we are, yet without sin" (Hebrews 4:15). When we face temptation, Jesus sympathizes with our weakness because he was tempted. Before he began public ministry, the Holy Spirit led him to the wilderness where the devil tempted him repeatedly.

Seeing that Jesus is alone and physically weak from fasting, the devil knows this is his opportunity to tempt Jesus. First, he entices Jesus to turn stones into bread. Since Jesus hasn't had food for forty days, the devil knows this temptation could have appeal. Jesus trusts God to sustain him. Next, the devil tries to persuade Jesus to do something spectacular, to throw himself over a cliff for a dramatic rescue by angels. Jesus discerns the devil's strategy to thwart God's plan for Jesus to redeem mankind by way of the cross. He refuses the devil, determined to fulfill God's spectacular plan. Lastly, the devil tries to seduce Jesus with power and authority in the world, with the condition that Jesus submit to him. Jesus will only submit to and worship God the Father (Matthew 4:1–11).

The devil's temptations hold a purpose: He wants to derail Jesus from completing God's purpose for him. Jesus discerns and withstands each temptation. He remains alert through his relationship with God. He knows the character of the Father. He knows the Word is Truth. He knows his purpose on earth.

The apostle Peter exhorts us to be alert as well. "Be sober-minded; be watchful. Your adversary the devil prowls around like a roaring lion, seeking someone to devour. Resist him, firm in your faith, knowing that the same kinds of suffering are being experienced by your brotherhood throughout the world" (1 Peter 5:8–9).

The devil knows that we have purposes that God intends to fulfill. He attempts to lure us away from growing in relationship with God. He does not want us to get to know God or pray—or we will experience that he is real and can help us. He does not want us to serve God with the gifts he has created in us. He especially does not want us to lead our children to know and love God through

Jesus, because they are the next generation of potentially powerful followers for Christ to further spread his kingdom.

We are most susceptible to temptation when we are tired, hurting, angry, distant from God, or removed from other believers. Our temptations don't usually look evil or wrong to us; they look appealing. The devil's strategy is that ". . . each person is tempted when he is lured and enticed by his own desire" (James 1:14). Personal temptations will be specific to our individual weaknesses and fleshly desires. For example, if we are starving for value, we may be tempted by commitments that will yield recognition. If we fear failure, we are more easily seduced to avoid exploring our abilities or considering new commitments. His aim is to lead us off God's designed path for us. Our greatest strength and defense is a strong and growing relationship with Jesus Christ.

SUBMIT

Jesus lived on earth for thirty-three years. He knew his purpose in this life, and he was committed to completing it. Death on the cross was in his near future, and he trusted God's promise to resurrect him from the dead for humankind's salvation. Jesus lived the ultimate submission—the Son of God humbled himself to become a human being. He submitted his will to the Father and trusted that his guidance would be perfect. Jesus walked through each day, ready to serve God at a moment's notice. He submitted and committed to the Father—even to his death.

During Jesus' three years of public ministry, crowds often followed him. They probably hoped he would teach one more time, answer one more question, or heal one more friend. All good works, right? Yet Jesus did not attend to every person because he did not answer to humanity. He knew when to rest—away from people. And he knew *how* to rest—with God. His eyes were fixed on the Father. Jesus was not a people pleaser, and he did not live to please himself. He lived for God alone.

God does not expect us to live as humbly as Jesus. He knows we are not perfect. God shows us the power of first-place love.

When we love Jesus most, everything else in our life gets in line behind him. Decisions and commitments are made through seeking him. We will mess up. But we will get back up, learn from our misstep, and return to him.

Jesus lived on earth and showed us how to live. Imagine the countless poor, needy, and sick whom he encountered. He loved them. Sometimes he remained with them and other times he moved on, in response to his Father's leading. He trusted God and believed that he held the larger plan. Sometimes we are called to walk away or say no. When this is a struggle, ask and trust God to meet the need.

When it was time to go to the cross, Jesus was troubled and prayed to God in the Garden of Gethsemane, expressing his desire to not do this. After he admitted his feelings and spent more time in prayer, he submitted fully to God's will. Whatever our hesitation or fear, we can share it with God. He faithfully equips us for whatever he wants us to do. God wants our life to be powerful. When we walk God's way, it will be.

Either we hold our life or we submit it. Both are decisions of the heart; one is selfish and the other is selfless. When we hold our life, we live our way, for ourself. When we submit our life, our first decision is to choose to trust God and the second is to try to follow his lead. One hour at a time, we learn to live for God like Jesus lived on earth for him. Whom do you live for?

"Dear God, Please transform my heart. Help me want to live for you. Amen."

FOLLOW

"If any of you wants to serve me, then follow me" (John 12:26a, MSG). Jesus says follow him—if we want to serve him. Otherwise, we lead or follow someone else. As we follow him, he shows us how to raise our children. He strengthens us to discern whether an opportunity is his plan, our preference, or someone else's plan for us. We serve him when we follow his guidance for determining each child's commitments. And as we teach them how to make commitments, we teach them how to follow Jesus.

"Then you'll be where I am, ready to serve at a moment's notice" (John 12:26b, MSG). Plenty of times I did not seek God and I did what I wanted. In the moment, the experience was gratifying, maybe even fun. Later on, I usually felt empty. Lots of empty experiences taught me that doing my own thing is not worth it.

Some ways we serve Jesus are hard or isolating, but when we experience God's peace, our heart settles because we know we are in his will. Other times a simple commitment of obedient service leaves us speechless, surprised by joy, or amazed by how fulfilled we are. Likewise, when we follow Jesus by saying no or stepping down, his peace quiets our heart or fills our void. The reward is sweet when we follow, but sometimes it's *hard* to stay the course. We might not like something we're involved in, or we want to do more. When you struggle, pray.

Practice: Prayer Starters for When We Struggle to Follow

- "Lord, I'm restless right now. Help me stay your course."
- "I'm confused. Please give me clarity."
- "I'm tired of _____. I give this to you. Fill me with your grace and strength."
- "I am intrigued by _____. I give this to you. Help me know if you are changing my course."

"Right now I am storm-tossed" (John 12:27a, MSG). Jesus relates to our self-doubt. Near to the cross, he admits this to God. Then he yields this to the Father and draws strength from him. We are to follow his example when self-doubt creeps into our heart: *How did I get in this situation? Why did I ever think I could do this?* God will attend our heart.

Live like Jesus. Remain alert—discern and reject temptation that lures you off God's path for you. Remain focused—you are loved and purposed by God. Jesus sympathizes with our weaknesses and will help us. Therefore, "Let us then with confidence draw near to the throne of grace, that we may receive mercy and find grace to help in time of need" (Hebrews 4:16).

THINK ABOUT IT

1. Why do you think it's so hard for us to yield to God the way we feel like living?

   a. Do you think he has the best plan for you? How about for your child?

2. Do you think you would become more peaceful if you felt like your decisions were inspired through prayer?

3. Temptations are intended to get you off course from what God has planned for you. Can you think of circumstances that you can now identify as possible temptations because they have detoured you at times?

   a. Can you identify a temptation for your child?

4. Sometimes our child believes that what he wants to do is fine, yet we know that it is not. We see the bigger picture and how his decision could affect him negatively or detour the best way forward for him. How is this scenario similar to how God teaches us to trust and follow him?

9

The Best Answer

PARENTS GIVE THE "FINAL word" to a child for every question of permission that she asks. If the source of our final word is God, his peace holds us when the child's reaction or experience is painful. If God is not our source, doubt and self-doubt grab every opportunity to hassle our heart.

Each *painful* memory I have of giving a child the answer that I believe God led me to is *covered* with a memory of God's faithfulness to the child and to our relationship. Sometimes his faithfulness displayed quickly, and other times much time passed. In his perfect time, God makes the goodness of his way known to both of us.

Often we say yes because we struggle to say no. It's easy to say yes. The child receives what he wants and we see that we have pleased him. Stay alert for opportunities to bless, even surprise, your child with this response. No is the hard answer to deliver, especially when we love the person to whom we say it. We know that our answer isn't what he wants; our answer might strain our relationship; and our answer may impact him among his peers. Often our no hurts our heart because we know something of the hurt that our child will endure. Our heart wrestles with what we should do.

Between the circumstance, the child's persistence, and sometimes other people, it's common to feel cornered and confused. Try to remember God is *right there* with you. He leads you, prepares the child, and follows through with his plan that is *always* bigger than the current circumstance that feels so big to our child and us. His peace will satisfy your soul.

Try this three-step approach for every circumstance: Ask God; discern his answer; say yes to him. You can do this. I know you can, with prayer and practice. Practice with the small stuff to grow prepared for the bigger questions down the road. Here we go.

ASK GOD

"I didn't see that coming."

"She always asks when I'm in the middle of something else, and I can't pull away to think about it."

"He springs it on me at the last minute . . . or when I'm at work . . . or in front of his friend . . . or when I'm exhausted . . . or with that adorable smile of his."

God knows the questions that are coming and when. He knows the condition of the relationship and sees the struggle in our heart. He is present to meet us at our point of need. "Draw near to God, and he will draw near to you" (James 4:8a).

Sometimes we have the opportunity to pull away and pray before we respond to a child. More often, we don't. Due to when they ask or what they ask, an answer tends to be needed in the moment.

"Can I go home with Jane?" (A text we receive just as the school day ends.)

"My favorite show comes on in an hour. Please can I watch it?" (Two hours ago, she complained of all the homework she has.)

"Everybody is going to see this movie. Can I go?" (His friend is on the phone, waiting to hear if our child needs a ride.)

A helpful step toward being prepared for impromptu questions is to invite God into your day and ask for his help. *God, I commit this day to you. Help me sense your guidance and follow you. Grow your wisdom in me. Amen.* Be intentional to pray like this throughout the day. It takes seconds. Set your watch or phone as a reminder until prayer is integrated into your day's rhythm.

God always provides the answer we need right on time. Our responsibility is to be present to him in order to discern his response. He helps us learn and assures us with his peace.

DISCERN GOD'S ANSWER

The Lord wants us to have confidence that we can discern his voice. Understanding how he communicates with you is a product of your personal relationship with him. "My sheep hear my voice, and I know them, and they follow me" (John 10:27). The more time we spend with someone, the better we know her. Engage with God while you fold laundry, work, cook supper, or run errands. Talk and practice listening. Sing worship songs to focus in his presence. Read his Word to learn his voice.

We can practice being in his presence anytime, anywhere.

SAY YES TO GOD

This takes courage and trust.

Our children were in elementary and middle school. A book series grew increasingly popular, and our kids wanted to read them. I prayed and yielded to God my personal opinion of the books. Within a few days, I sensed that God's answer was no regarding the books. Each time I imagined telling them no, I pictured my children's pained faces. I prayed again . . . and again. I had no sense of God's peace to say yes to my children.

Personally, I was relieved by God's answer, but the pain in my heart gripped me. My children had some hard days ahead. No meant that when their friends talked about one of the books, my children would feel left out. No meant that when a book's movie came out, our children couldn't go. No meant facing their peers' question: *Why can't you read it?* And no meant facing the temptation to sneak behind my back to read it anyway: *Just read it at school; your parents won't ever know.*

Every time a new book or movie in the series came out, it was hard for our kids, but they got through it. In fact, they more than "got through it," because God built endurance in their hearts as they persevered. He uses everything to accomplish his bigger purposes in his bigger plan.

Looking back, the books were simply one example of a recurring theme—the opportunity to practice asking God, discerning his answer, and saying yes to him. Additionally, I hoped and prayed that our children would observe and eventually apply this principle in their life.

Sometimes it was hard to not give in to a child's confusion or another parent's attitude. God gave me courage to say what he wanted me to say. I felt his strength and grace to respond to parents when they asked me why I would not allow my child to watch or participate in something with "everyone." He grew my trust in him—to believe that he holds my relationship with each child, that he sees the long view, and he knows what is best for each of them.

When we say yes to God, we demonstrate that he is Lord of our life—which includes our role as mom. We experience his faithfulness. Pray for his help and courage.

Practice: Go to God for Answers

1. Ask God, by presenting the question or issue and your concerns: "I give this to you. What is your answer?"

2. Discern his answer: "Please help me hear you and confirm your answer somehow."

3. Say yes to God. Give God your concerns: "Thank you for your answer. Please prepare her heart and protect her. Protect our relationship. Help me say this your way. Help me love her well and walk through this with grace."

WHY IS IT SO HARD TO SAY NO?

Sometimes we have a hard time telling someone no because we worry about the person's reaction. The root of worry is fear.

"I am afraid he will be mad at me."

"I am afraid that I won't be able to control her when she reacts."

"I don't want to disappoint him."

"I am worried about what the other moms will think."

"I am worried about how she will be treated at school."

Name your fear or worry and release it to God. If you realize that you draw worth and value from the person, release that too. Ask God to fill this emptied place in your heart with his comforting love. When our worth and value are established in God's love for us, his peace permeates our heart. We trust he will carry us through hard conversations and relationships.

Jesus' closest followers placed all relationships behind their relationship with him. They loved their family, but committed their life to Jesus. "And everyone who has left houses or brothers or sisters or father or mother or children or lands, for my name's sake, will receive a hundredfold and will inherit eternal life" (Matthew 19:29). Jesus understands the pain we may experience. Some people will be gracious; others will not. He promises immense blessing for those who live for him.

Sometimes no can be avoided. Pray in advance about a season that is on the horizon. Consider and implement boundaries that you can predict will surface soon. Plan conversations with your child rather than have conversations in the heated moment.

Build a healthy relationship so that you and your child understand one another better.

Practice: Pray in Advance

1. Relationship: "Lord, show me how to nurture this relationship. Protect all that is healthy and strengthen what is weak. Grow us together, with you at the center. Amen."

2. Season or decision: "Help me know which activities each child should be involved in. Please prepare this in them."

3. Friends: "Bring your friends for our children."

4. Boundaries: "Help me know what boundaries I need to have in place regarding clothes, television, and privileges."

TEACHING A CHILD TO GO TO GOD

When we teach our child to pursue God's answer, she learns that he is our true "final word" for our decisions and our final word when we make decisions regarding her. When decisions remain solely between our child and us, we invite the possibility of going round and round with a question—until we are worn out and give in. As the child prays and we pray, God knits our hearts in peace and builds our relationship.

Age four is a good starting age to begin to pray with your child about things he wants or wants to do. *Dear Jesus, I want a truck like my friend's truck. Please help me know if I should have it now.* If your child is a preteen or teen, ask God to prepare the child's heart to want to pray. *Lord, please open his heart to talk to you about things like this, and help him wait for and learn to discern your answer.* Express interest to be involved. *Hey, if you ever want to share how you think God is leading you, I would love to hear. If not, I understand. I'm praying for you to hear.*

When we pray with or separately for our child, the final decision expressed to the child is ours. We are God's appointed authority figure in his life, and hopefully our decision is informed through prayer.

Our response to a child sometimes leads to temporary strain or anger between us. This makes sense—the child is not getting what he wants. Pray for his heart and for the relationship. Recall when you were his age in order to appreciate some of his struggle. Draw on God's grace and walk with him through his learning curve. God faithfully leads us through. He is always up to far more than we see.

A Story

One day Cecilia, age nine, came home from school and described a pair of tennis shoes that several of her friends had. She really wanted a pair—so much so that she learned which stores sold them and the cost. I explained that the cost was considerably more than we usually spend on shoes. She pressed. I repeated. Off and on for the rest of the day, Cecilia appealed from different angles. Exhausted with the topic, I offered, "If you are willing to pray about it, then I will too." When Cecilia was younger, we prayed together; gradually she moved toward preferring to pray by herself. We agreed that after a few days we would share from our individual prayers and then pray together.

Those few days were interesting. I wrestled with the issue of paying so much for a pair of shoes that my daughter would outgrow in less than a year, and I fretted. *Four other mothers bought the silly shoe. Am I making too big of a deal of this? Will she feel left out if I don't buy her this shoe? What will this do to our relationship? Ugh!*

I released these thoughts to God several times and sought his guidance. Two days later I saw the brilliant silver lining: My daughter was willing to release her desire to God and ask him what she should do. Also, during our days of prayer, Cecilia did not once mention the shoes to me. She could have said, "Momma, I really want these shoes! I hope your answer is yes!" Instead, all her conversation about the shoes was with God.

When we talk or vent to God, he attends our heart. This is the power of prayer.

We met in her room and sat on the floor facing each other between her twin beds. "Did you hear anything?" I softly asked. Shaking her head, she asked the same question. We each tried to suppress a smile when we admitted that we did not hear anything even though we prayed a lot. I was amazed by Cecilia's calm and the absence of strain between us. The sweet atmosphere displayed God's influence on our hearts through our prayers.

Still, I was unsure about God's direction regarding the shoes. I prayed silently, *God, I trust you to lead this. My girl is really looking to you to answer her. I need you to move strongly right now.*

"Okay, Sweetie, we each know what we want, and we have both given this to the Lord. God is glad about that. Why don't we pray the same prayers together that we have prayed alone? Then, let's just be quiet and wait for God to speak to us. He wants us to get our answer from him—which means he will answer us. Maybe it will be today and maybe it won't. I'll go first."

I then prayed, "Dear Jesus, You know that I am not peaceful about buying these shoes. I give my feelings to you. If you want Cecilia to have them, help me to know this."

Cecilia prayed, "Dear Jesus, I really want the tennis shoes like all my friends have. I know they cost a lot. I give you what I want. Please tell me if I can have these shoes."

Eyes closed, we sat in silence for several minutes. I had the thought that we could find a similar pair of shoes for less but I could not discern whether this was my idea or God answering me. However, I clearly sensed that God wanted Cecilia to know his answer, so I waited.

"Are you hearing anything, Cecilia?"

Looking at me with tears in her eyes, she responded, "I don't think I am supposed to have them." Immediately, my tears overflowed. Love for her overwhelmed my heart, as I hurt for her pain and admired her devotion to God. My little girl heard God give her an answer that she had hoped against, and she chose in the moment to share his will with me and obey him. God grew her heart and *their* relationship. The shoes were merely the attention-getter.

I have wondered if my emotional reaction to Cecilia's tears and submission to God was a tiny glimpse of how our heavenly Father feels when he tells us no, knows exactly how difficult accepting his answer will be, and hears us say yes to him. God is always at work in the heart of both the child and parent.

"Let's pray some more because I believe the Lord has more to tell you."

After several minutes Cecilia said she saw the name of a store, so we agreed to go shopping on Saturday to see if the right shoe for her was there. At the store she found a shoe similar one that she pictured that day we prayed. She squealed, "Momma, this is the shoe that Jesus wants me to have!"

God transformed heartbreak to heart growth.

Trust God's No

It is easier to give our child what they want, that's for sure. I think God tells us yes far more than he tells us no. Likewise, we can provide more opportunities in which our child experiences yes. As circumstances arise, we teach and encourage our child to surrender her desire to God and ask him for guidance. Believe that God will take it from there. He works through our discussions, training, and prayers in ways that we may not see.

As we pray, he is already at work in our heart and our child's heart. He gives grace to us to help us trust him, to submit to his will, and to inspire our heart for the conversation with the child. He gives grace to our child and prepares her to hear the answer. This doesn't mean there is no pain or challenge. It means God is with us and will carry us through the circumstance.

Pray steadfastly for your child and yourself to discern God's answer, and pray that you will be faithful to him and full of grace with your child. A child may react strongly when we say no. Sometimes this is because he truly doesn't understand or agree with our reason. Other times, our reasons make sense, but he reacts to not getting his way. Even as adults, we react sometimes when we don't get our way. When we react, God loves us through that moment.

God answers us firmly, with grace and love. He gives us space and boundaries for our reaction to his answer. This is how we are to love our child.

It's not so much about a desired item or opportunity—God wants us to draw near. He wants us to get comfortable talking—and listening. He wants us to know him. God wants our child to believe he is real and relate with him.

THINK ABOUT IT

1. Have you answered yes or no when you knew you the opposite response would be wiser?

   a. What was the overall effect on you?

   b. What was the overall effect on the child?

   c. What was your reason?

2. As God's steward of our child, why do you suppose God hopes we will seek him for how to respond to our child?

3. Have you experienced relationship strain with a child because your response wasn't the child's preference, though it was a result of listening for God's leading? Did you experience peace, even in the trial?

4. Do you struggle to say no to your child?

   a. If so, when or under what conditions?

   b. Has saying no to your child ever ultimately resulted in blessing her? How?

5. How do you think your no tends to be received—as firm yet gentle, timid and worried, or harsh?

6. Do you tend to give in when your child whines, has a fit, or gives you the silent treatment? Why?

7. Have you considered praying for your child when your answer is no?

10

When Things Get Out of Whack

FROM TIME TO TIME, my husband and I let our priorities get jumbled. The shift is gradual. Small commitments made without prayer pile up. Time given to new projects or activities is not monitored. We are less intentional about planning and protecting time with each other and as a family.

We have learned that when one of our priorities is out of whack, someone in our home suffers. For example, if one of us neglects time with the Lord, we are prone to react rather than thoughtfully respond to each other. When work or volunteer hours are out of balance, disconnectedness is felt in the marriage or with a child. Typically, we don't recognize our own imbalance. Our spouse or the child *experiences* it.

When our boys were toddlers, they seldom saw their daddy, and when I saw him, he was spent. Terrell loved us deeply, but he was not home much. Twelve-hour workdays had become his norm. I was exhausted and angry, and the boys missed their daddy. For months I cried, nagged, and complained, and every now and then I whined a prayer. When I realized drama was a waste of time, I began to pray more. Basically, I poured out to God, over and over again, how he needed to get Terrell's attention. I was surprised when he seemed to shift my prayer focus. God led me to unload to him my hurt, anger, and judgment toward Terrell. As days passed, God's grace moved me to forgive Terrell in my heart. Part of me did not want to because this meant releasing him from resentment that I held tightly. As I forgave, my thoughts about Terrell became prayers for his heart. I prayed that he would see what God wants him to see—just like he led me to see what I needed to see.

Following much conversation and prayer, God healed our marriage. A heart change was necessary for each of us. God led us to establish order for our priorities. We had learned the hard way that this influences how we determine and manage commitments—which affects the measure of peace in our hearts and home.

Top priorities include our personal relationship with Jesus, our marriage (if married), and our children. All other priorities follow these. Periodically, other priorities may require more time. God hopes we seek his way through such seasons and not devise our own.

We communicate value through how we relegate time—time that God gives us. How we live the day reflects the true order of our priorities. When we say our relationship with Jesus comes first, our family witnesses this. Our character is transformed because we open our heart to the effect of his Word and we practice depending on him in prayer. Change may not be profound, but effort is visible. The priority of our marriage and children is evidenced in the quality of these relationships. Additionally, our children learn about priorities from how they experience ours. Our actions tell the story.

RECOGNIZE THE CHALLENGE

Stating priority standards is a good first step. Living them out is hard.

I have been a stay-at-home mom, worked full-time and part-time, and officed at home and away from home. As a stay-at-home mom, I juggled a full schedule of volunteer commitments in some seasons, while other times I sensed I was to keep my commitments very simple. It's easy to become the stay-at-home mom who is seldom at home, or we can pour so much energy into the home and our children that we have nothing left for our husband.

When I returned to employment, I began each day with a firm boundary for when to leave the office. There was always so much to get done and not enough time to do it— just like at home. My family held first place in my heart, however, the decisions that I made shouted that work mattered more than my family. For example, I came home from the office or left my home office when the school day ended, but I let work themes occupy my thoughts. Sadly, I was partly present to my children and partly present to work. Too often once the children turned to their homework or went to bed, I resumed a work project on my computer and ignored the opportunity to be with Terrell.

Every day I completed the essentials for home and work, and this relief camouflaged the absence of peace in my heart and home. When our priorities are messed up, we tend to eventually erupt, though it takes us a while to figure out why. Exasperated thoughts, tears, or outbursts often reveal something is out of whack:

I have got too much going on.

The kids have too much going on.

Something has got to change soon!

At first I did not realize my priorities were mixed up. My husband did. He broached the subject more gently than I had with him years earlier, and he understood well the challenge before me to adjust my pattern.

My return to work was a big change for our family and for me. Any big change is reason to consider in advance how to remain strong with our priority standards. It is wise to watch for how each family member adjusts and how relationships and routines are affected.

JESUS FIRST

Jesus knows how easily people, passions, and self-absorption can become our primary focus. He is clear: Relationship with him should be our primary pursuit. He assures us that he will attend our other concerns.

> Therefore do not be anxious, saying, "What shall we eat?" or "What shall we drink?" or "What shall we wear?" For the Gentiles seek after all these things, and your heavenly Father knows that you need them all. But seek first the kingdom of God and his righteousness, and all these things will be added to you. (Matthew 6:31–33)

As we spend time with the Lord, he strengthens us to be present to him through the day wherever we are. When we decide that Jesus is our first priority, he becomes the cornerstone for every relationship we have. He is our solid foundation on which to live.

> Everyone then who hears these words of mine and does them will be like a wise man who built his house on the rock. And the rain fell, the floods came, and the winds blew and beat on that house, but it did not fall, because it had been founded on the rock. And everyone who hears these words of mine and does not do them will be like a foolish man who built his house on sand. And the rain fell, the floods came, and the winds blew and beat against that house, and it fell, and great was the fall of it. (Matthew 7:24–27)

When *we* try to design our life, what we build will not stand through the storms of life. We live strong when we submit to Jesus' building design.

MARRIAGE SECOND

God intends that marriage is our most intimate human relationship. "Therefore a man shall leave his father and his mother and hold fast to his wife, and the two shall become one flesh" (Genesis 2:24). No other human relationship is given the directive to "become one." God does not tell us "become one" with our parent, a sibling, a child, or a best friend.

God desires to knit husband and wife together emotionally, spiritually, and physically. If you are married, this means you are to be God's most significant vessel of his love to your husband. God knows our love capabilities and to what degree we love each other when we get married. He gives us love with which to love our husband, and he intends that we experience the same from him. He has plans to grow us close and mold our relationship toward oneness.

God designed our husband and us, yet his fulfillment of our design is shaped throughout our lives. We think we know our mate, but how can we if we are continually being shaped by God? As God grows each of us, he desires to grow our marriage too. Are we participating with him? Is this a priority to us?

> He answered, "Have you not read that he who created them from the beginning made them male and female, and said, 'Therefore a man shall leave his father and his mother and hold fast to his wife, and the two shall become one flesh'? So they are no longer two but one flesh. What therefore God has joined together, let not man separate." (Matthew 19:4–6)

Jesus declares the significance of the vow we make when we marry. In this passage, he quotes from Genesis and attributes the words to God. He underlines the importance of oneness in marriage. God has joined us, and we are not to let man separate us. Do we work to have a strong union? Do we live joined as one—or do we live as two?

Prioritizing our marriage is very hard work. We need God's power and love to accomplish this. It is important to intentionally secure time to talk and enjoy one another. Mixing up our priorities tends to happen gradually. Prayer is essential. When our relationship is healthy—and especially when it is not—we need to pray for each other. When you struggle, talk to God. Ask him when and how to share your feelings with your spouse. Pray for healing, for grace to forgive, and for grace to wait for God's timing. Believe that God hears you and works to accomplish his purposes.

Our marriage impacts the atmosphere of the home and the cohesiveness of the entire family. It influences each child's disposition and sense of security.

CHILDREN THIRD

God's plan for the family provides expression for his love to mankind. Our love toward a child is to reflect God's love as our heavenly Father. This love is full, yet includes discipline. A godly marriage reflects Christ's love for his church. Christ is the bridegroom and the church is his bride. (Ephesians 5:22–33) God intends our child to witness our marriage as an earthly example for how Christ loves the church through a deep abiding union.

> Children, obey your parents in the Lord, for this is right. "Honor your father and mother" (this is the first commandment with a promise), "that it may go well with you and that you may live long in the land." (Ephesians 6:1–3)

The apostle Paul succinctly specifies honor toward God, the responsibility of parents to lead, and the command to children to obey their parents. He refers to God's command "Honor your father and your mother, that your days may be long in the land that the LORD your God is giving you" (Exodus 20:12). Unity of the parents in their leadership is inferred. This develops over time, as each parent grows in the Lord. Oneness in marriage strengthens parents to pray and discuss details of raising their children. When children observe solidarity in the marriage, they experience the security of one consistent message from their parents.

If you are a single mom, God walks closely with you. Seek him to fill all voids for your children and for you.

The biblical order of priorities is clear. Yet our children often receive more attention than our spouse. This happens for a variety of reasons:

- We experienced this pattern when we grew up.

- Our marriage is strained. Rather than confront our issues, we focus on our children.

- A child's need is more visible than our spouse's. Without thinking, we attend to the child first.

- A child requires extra attention for behavioral reasons, special needs, or a health issue. We lose track of time and have little or nothing left to give to our spouse.

- The guidance in these Bible verses is new for us.

Cultivating this balance is especially difficult in blended families. The parents need to teach and reorder the children's understanding of the priority of the marriage. Prayer, gentleness, loving assurance, and time help this transition.

God knows our circumstance and wants to lead us through. When we pursue and obey him, our marriage and relationships with our children will attest to his faithfulness to us. As we try to obey his order, his peace fills our heart, each child's heart, and our home.

EVERYBODY ELSE

The family is precious to God. Our quality of care to our family precedes our other involvements. How we lead and manage them demonstrates their place of value in our heart. In turn, this will reflect in our management ability elsewhere. "If anyone does not know how to manage his own family, how can he take care of God's church?" (1 Timothy 3:5, NIV). A person's capability to manage his family is used to measure his capacity to lead within God's church.

Sometimes work, a significant relationship, or a project we believe we are called to fulfill will require a greater measure of our time. This may last a couple of weeks or for an extended season. Pray for your family and for yourself and depend on God's guidance and insights. Continue to be intentional about priority relationships even though the configuration is different. Strategically plan and communicate change to the family.

Aim to follow the Lord's lead. He knows each heart and shows us how to participate with him to give time and attention where it is needed. For example: If you temporarily work a night shift, shift your quiet time and schedule appointed times to be with family. If a new work project requires several months of late nights or travel, mark the calendar with phone, coffee, and evening dates with your spouse. Plan time with the kids. Communicate more during the day with quick calls and texts. A handwritten note can be read repeatedly. Be flexible with meal times to provide time for the family around the table. If a family member requires extra attention such that the regular routine is disrupted (surgery, new weekly appointments, travel to help a loved one), pray for grace for everyone and express gratitude for supportive attitudes.

The following questions highlight our strengths and weaknesses regarding effort toward work, community, and family. As you answer, take time to thank God for progress and to ask for his continued help to live into strong commitment standards.

Practice: Priorities Check-Up

1. Which (work, community, or family) gets my best energy?

2. Which (work, community, or family) seems to be on my mind the most?

3. Which relationships (work, community, or family) are healthiest?

4. Do I strategically plan and guard quality time with my family the way that I mark my calendar for work and other involvements?

5. Compared to two months ago, which (work, community, or family) is clearly moving forward for the better?

Perhaps you grew up with a different value system. God leads and empowers us as we turn to him. Name and release your feelings, thoughts, and desires to God. He responds and molds our heart.

Practice: Prayer to Reorder Priorities

1. Describe the order you want to change and release: "God, I realize my priorities are out of order. I spend too much time _____. I neglect _____. I release my order for priorities to you."

2. Ask for God's forgiveness. He loves you and forgives you.

3. Name desired changes and invite help: "Jesus, I want you to have first place in my life. Please help me and show me your steps forward. Thank you."

4. Pray for healing: "Please heal and restore _____."

CONCLUSION

The apostle Peter loved Jesus deeply and publicly voiced passionate commitment to him. Yet he denied Jesus three times right before he went to the cross. Jesus knew the state of Peter's heart and still loved him deeply.

Peter struggled through the humbling realization of his weakness, yet God used his humbled state to shape his heart to become a deeply faithful servant. After his resurrection, Jesus asks Peter three times if he loved him. Humbled, changed, and even more passionately committed to Jesus, Peter professes his love. Knowing Peter's heart, Jesus extends a tremendous call to Peter to tend his sheep. Later, Peter would write to the church:

> Tend the flock of God that is your charge, not by constraint but willingly, not for shameful gain but eagerly, not as domineering over those in your charge but being examples to the flock. And when the chief Shepherd appears, you will receive the unfading crown of glory. (1 Peter 5:2–4, RSV)

You and I are shepherds, and our flock is our children. We are to tend our flock "willingly" and "eagerly." As we try to walk the way of God's Word, the Good Shepherd shows us how to shepherd.

THINK ABOUT IT

1. Which relational priorities do you tend to jumble?

   a. Why do you think this happens?

2. How do you think your other priorities could be strengthened if you place your relationship with Jesus first?

3. Do you think that your order for priorities impacts how your children will order theirs?

4. Consider ways that you balance commitments with:

   a. Extended family

   b. Friends

   c. Work

   d. Ministry and community service

   e. Oh, and time for you!

PART FOUR

The Power of Forgiveness

11

We Don't Know What
We Are Missing

"A HARVEST OF RIGHTEOUSNESS is sown in peace by those who make peace" (James 3:18).

The peaceful mom seeks to partner with God in every dimension of her life. God responds and steadfastly pours peace into her heart. She knows forgiveness is God's gift to her. She applies his gift to her own heart and to each relationship within her family. She explains God's gift to her children and helps them receive it as their own.

This section unfolds how we "make peace" with God and in our home. When we partner with God and sow the practice of forgiveness in our home, he gives growth that we might, in peace, *raise a harvest of righteousness.*

When our children lived with us, at some point in the week or even on multiple days, there was conflict—misunderstanding, hurt feelings, a disagreement, or expressed jealousy. The conflict might be between one of the children and me, between my husband and me, or between two of the children. We loved each other, and actually liked each other a lot; we enjoyed doing things together. But plenty of times we did not seen eye to eye on things—nap times, habits, meal choices, clothing and hair preferences, who sits where in the car, whose turn it is for anything, or house rules and responsibilities.

Inadvertently, and sometimes intentionally, we hurt one another. We tease, don't include someone, call names, or make comments that tear down rather than build up. In addition, each of us periodically has life issues that affect how we relate with other family members—fatigue, the condition of our self-esteem (from overconfident and bossy to insecure and jealous), or working through relationships and circumstances outside the home.

For all the conflict, hurt, and individual issues we have had, we are a very close family. A key reason for this is the power of forgiveness.

How powerful is forgiveness? Forgiveness restores, builds, and strengthens relationships. It reflects selflessness as we release what we think we deserve for the sake of the relationship. It demonstrates love for God and for the individual. As we forgive others, God's love grows in us.

God forgave us through the sacrifice of his Son Jesus to redeem our life and restore our access to relationship with him. His forgiveness is grace—underserved merit founded on immeasurable and perfect love. It is so powerful that as our personal relationship with Jesus grows, the outpour of his grace overflows from us to those we love. His example to love us by choosing to forgive us inspires us to *choose* to give forgiveness.

Conflict and hurt affect many relationships. Forgiveness exposes the best of our character and inspires us to pursue healthier relationships. Unfortunately, we struggle to seek it, give it, and receive it. We often behave like children when it comes to admitting our wrongs, holding grudges, licking our wounds, or genuinely forgiving.

When our boys were three and four years old, they played together like bear cubs. They moved inseparably from one small adventure to the next, sharing their imaginations. Sharing a toy was not as easy. This challenge occurred daily. Some days Terrell would claim a toy—"I'm playin' wif this truck today, Ellison"—or tell his brother that he needed the *very* toy that Ellison was playing with and take it. Ellison, fifteen months younger, adored his big brother. He wanted every toy that intrigued Terrell, so whenever the opportunity presented, he would attempt to take the toy from where Terrell had put it, to discover what fascinated his hero so much. Of course, each reacted when the other was the aggressor by calling to me, crying, or taking care of the matter in his own aggressive way.

Sometimes we settled the issue quickly, but often the boys got physical. When this happened, the following day Terrell would proclaim to Ellison, "I'm playin' wif the truck *by myself*," or early in the morning Ellison would dash to get the toy that was Terrell's favorite the day before and go play with it in a private place. The boys demonstrated that their hurt, anger, or impatience could accumulate. I realized it was time to teach the boys about forgiveness.

IS THE TIME IT TAKES WORTH IT?

Forgiveness is challenging to teach and practice because the need for it surfaces all day long. Our child is on a massive learning curve for a lot of hours each day. Many of those hours reflect obedience, and we need to remember this. In other hours we deal with disobedience, lies, hurt, meanness, or disrespect. We are challenged to be consistent to follow through with the consequence we announced in our warning. After we compose ourself to deal with the misbehavior and remember what that consequence was, it is tempting to stop there. Don't. Do not deprive your child or yourself of the game-changing effect that forgiveness gradually—or sometimes immediately—accomplishes.

Some days we are met with repetitive misbehavior or a child's unwillingness to forgive or to ask forgiveness. This weakens our enthusiasm to incorporate forgiveness into our family relationships. We are also personally faced with decisions of forgiveness: Our child hurts or disobeys us; we hurt or mistreat a child. We may struggle to forgive our child, grapple with being humble to admit to God (and perhaps our child) our wrong, or find it hard to ask a child for forgiveness.

We desperately need God, the Author of forgiveness, to establish this discipline in our child's heart and ours. He commands us to forgive. With him, we can. With him, we can train our child to forgive. With him, our family can enjoy healthy relationships.

Forgiveness challenges us throughout our lives. We experience hurt, betrayal, rejection, or other offenses within and outside our family. Likewise, we hurt and offend others, though we don't like to admit it. In both scenarios, we are faced with the decision to forgive, seek forgiveness, and receive forgiveness—or not. Our child struggles with the same decisions.

Sometimes we forget how young she is and how little practice she has really had, or we do not consider how much older we are and how long we have struggled at times regarding forgiveness. The child's forgiveness-issue-of-the-moment may seem straightforward to us, but to her it is challenging, just as our personal forgiveness matters are to us. When we humbly consider our lifelong learning curve, perhaps compassion and understanding will swell in our heart and strengthen us to help, rather than judge, our child as she learns.

In the midst of training our children about forgiveness, I was humbled many times by my weakness and inconsistency to live what I taught. We honor God as we try to apply his teaching to our life and then pass his teaching on to our children. Often we learn alongside them, which is a powerful reminder of the level ground we walk with them.

A relationship can die a slow death if forgiveness is absent. Many parent/child and sibling relationships are built on unresolved hurts and offenses. Left unchecked, these harden into feelings like resentment, judgment, bitterness, or rejection. For instance, when a child lashes out at the parent, or the parent lashes out at the child, or a sibling lashes out at a sibling, this is often due to suppressed or hardened wounds lodged in memory. Strained or broken relationships can be restored through acts of forgiveness. Someone needs to *seek* forgiveness; someone needs to *give* forgiveness; and the seeker needs to *receive* that he is forgiven.

"The tongue has the power of life and death" (Proverbs 18:21a, NIV). Words of forgiveness are words of life.

ETIQUETTE OR LIFE SKILL?

Mom: "Say you're sorry."

Child: "I'm sorry."

Sound familiar? The child complies because he wants to return to what he was doing—which may eventually include what he was doing to bother his sister. "I'm sorry" is what many of us (and our children) are taught to say when we offend someone or disobey. We understand it as another etiquette phrase, like "please" or "thank you," to demonstrate thoughtfulness and respect. Do we want our children to understand forgiveness as two more words of etiquette? Or do we want them to understand it as a powerful experience of humility, honesty, release, love, healing, and reconciliation?

We can teach a child to say what he is sorry for and ask for forgiveness. When he does, he is learning how to be humble and honest, and to demonstrate value for someone. It's very hard to say, "I am sorry that I ____. Will you forgive me?" When the child does, even if he struggles to mean it, God responds to his willingness and grows the practice of forgiveness and these traits in his heart. For it is God's desire that we learn to forgive with such traits. When the other person says, "I forgive you," release is given and experienced. God responds and blesses the relationship with love, healing, and reconciliation.

Our intent is key. It will influence the passion behind our teaching and training. As you read this chapter, consider what forgiveness means to you.

Forgiveness is at the heart of the gospel. It is the message that God wants us to embrace, practice, and pass to our children by example and discipleship. Until we consider the power of forgiveness, *we don't know what we are missing.*

WHAT DO WE BELIEVE, REALLY?

What has your personal experience with forgiveness been like over the years? Someone said she forgave you, but she does not act like she has let go of the offense. Maybe you are struggling to forgive a family member until he admits his mistake. Or, you told your sister you forgave her a long time ago, but deep down you still hold a grudge. Our experiences with people are very different from how God says he forgives.

> He does not deal with us according to our sins, nor repay us according to our iniquities. For as high as the heavens are above the earth, so great is his steadfast love toward those who fear him; as far as the east is from the west, so far does he remove our transgressions from us. (Psalm 103:10–12)

This is God's truth. Do you believe these words?

Our answer impacts how we integrate forgiveness within our family—the degree to which we seek, give, and receive forgiveness. God knows we initially view his forgiveness through the lens of our personal experiences of conflict and attempted reconciliation with significant people in our life. More often we treat each other or give payback according to how we feel about what the person did or neglected to do.

God's Word says that his love for his children is so greatly unwavering that he removes our sin as far as is possible. These are powerful words for which we need powerful faith. We need to take God at his Word.

Our sin and shame may haunt us, and we know that we do not deserve mercy. Once we realize what God did for us when he gave Jesus to die on the cross to save us and restore the privilege of relationship with him, the concept of his love for us is overwhelming. This evidence of his love inspires us to try to love in every manner he commands. His love becomes our strength to say yes to him and obey him.

If you struggle to believe or receive God's forgiveness, ask him to help you. God knows you, your experiences, and how you process things. He can show you how to participate with him to remove obstacles that prevent you from enjoying his forgiveness. Read Scripture about forgiveness to learn of God's patience with humankind and how thorough his forgiveness is. When we read and reflect, God helps us see how similar our sin is to theirs. Our trust in him grows through the stories of lives changed by his forgiveness. As our heart softens, we forgive and seek forgiveness to demonstrate to God our love for him.

"But God shows his love for us in that while we were still sinners, Christ died for us" (Romans 5:8). Forgiveness is the primary means through which God demonstrates his love and desire for relationship with *you*.

BEGIN

For healthy practice to take root, plant seeds. God gives growth. In faith, believe God. In faith, teach and train. In faith, pray often that each child grows to understand the forgiveness she has been given in Christ and the forgiveness she extends toward others.

Practice: Prayers to Be a Family Who Forgives

- Please grow a willing and teachable heart in _____.
- Help him learn to come to you for forgiveness when he offends.
- Help her learn to come to you for help to forgive others.
- Give grace to (name) to help him ask for forgiveness, give forgiveness, and receive forgiveness within his family.
- Help me discern your opportunities to teach and train about forgiveness. Please give me your words and anointing.
- Fill me with your strength, patience, and passion to persevere when I am discouraged and tired.

- Grow me to genuinely practice forgiveness toward others and to be an authentic witness for my children.

- Please restore our family relationships, especially where we have not practiced forgiveness.

Whether a child is five or fifteen, we have the privilege to lay a foundation that can benefit and bless our child for the rest of her life and for eternity. God knows when you or your child first learn about or realize the significance of forgiveness. He sees your willing heart and lovingly works his plan.

Read an age-appropriate translation of the gospel message to your child and ask him to express what he understands. Even four-year-olds can begin to understand a very simple version of Jesus' life, death, and resurrection. Here is an example of the gospel message simplified for a very young child:

God loves us so much. One day he told his son Jesus to leave heaven and go live with people like you and me for a while, so that we could learn about God and heaven. God told Jesus that one day he would have to die on a cross for all the times everybody has ever disobeyed, including you and me. Jesus loves us so much, so he obeyed God and did this for everyone. It was a very sad day when Jesus died on the cross. But three days later, God made Jesus to be alive again! Now he is alive and back in heaven with God. Jesus did all this so that whenever we disobey, God forgives us. And when God forgives us, he also decides to forget what we did wrong.

Wise discipleship requires that we use language and examples they can understand. For example, instead of using the word "sin," we said, "when you disobey," "when you are mean," "when you don't tell the truth." As a child gets older, modify vocabulary, detail, and depth to describe why Jesus came and how this impacts our life. Christian children's books, Bibles, and videos aid us with age-appropriate materials. God uses our words and marks the child's heart with understanding that suits his age.

How we practice forgiveness with a child affects her view of God's forgiveness. If we want the child to believe God means what he says about forgiveness, our example needs to reflect his example. For instance, we seek God's forgiveness for a repetitive pattern of disobedience, such as jealousy, and we are encouraged to persevere because we know he forgives us. Hopefully, in like manner, we will extend forgiveness to our child as she struggles to overcome a repetitive pattern of disobedience, such as talking back.

When we humbly consider willful patterns of our life, this can positively affect our perspective toward a child's willful journey. Our age at the time of our willful struggle does not matter. What matters is that we realize we stand on level ground with our child as a sinner. Memories of God's mercy and patience through our struggles inspire us to reflect his character as we walk with our child.

The apostle Paul walked this balance with those in his sphere of influence. In Acts 26:1–29 he shares his story. First, Paul (whose name was Saul before he met Jesus) reflects on his past sin, describing how he murdered many Christians. Then he tells how Jesus met him on the road and confronted him about his sin. Knowing Jesus could have judged him there, Paul was transformed by the power of Jesus' love and forgiveness. To further demonstrate the fullness of his forgiveness, Jesus gave Paul a mission to spread the gospel. Through God's powerful love, Paul lived passionately for Jesus and the spread of the gospel. He humbly counted himself a fellow sinner saved by grace. "To this day I have had the help that comes from God" (Acts 26:22a).

Our children will receive plenty of practice from both sides of forgiveness—as the offender and the offended. Their experiences and other broken relationships they observe provide ample examples for discussion and training. They witness the benefits of reconciliation and the consequences of stubbornness or a hardened heart. When a child apologizes or speaks words of forgiveness, we cannot see what she truly feels in her heart. We do not need to; God sees the heart and works his purposes through her willingness to participate in forgiveness. He uses what we plant and sow, and one day we will discover all that he has grown.

THINK ABOUT IT

1. Do you stop to consider how many times during the day that your child is actually doing what you prefer? Try to notice this more often and be encouraged.

2. Do you pray for God's help, for your child and for yourself, to be strengthened to practice forgiveness? Take a minute now and do this. Think of a time early in your morning to mark as a moment to pray this daily. Copy the prayer list in this chapter and tape it to your bathroom mirror.

3. Do you struggle to receive God's forgiveness? Look up "forgiveness" in the back of your Bible and read some of the passages about it. Pray for God's help.

12

Learning to Forgive

ONE AMAZING WAY THAT God displays his power is through acts of forgiveness. He lifts burden or wound from our heart when we admit our fault or release someone from her offense toward us. He grows humility in us and cares for the heart of the person who hears our humble words. He heals and restores both hearts and builds a strong foundation for the relationship. "The God of our fathers raised Jesus, whom you killed by hanging him on a tree. God exalted him at his right hand as Leader and Savior, to give repentance to Israel and forgiveness of sins" (Acts 5:30–31). The apostle Peter seizes the moment before an angry council to proclaim how God raised Jesus from the dead to "give" us forgiveness for our sins. God's forgiveness covers our lifespan of sin and opens heaven's gate to us. Never could we deserve or earn such immeasurable love and grace.

God generously gives his forgiveness and hopes we receive it. As his love washes our heart, he desires that we love him with all our heart, soul, mind, and strength. We demonstrate our love for him when we obey him and love others with his love. One way we love others is through forgiveness.

A healthy relationship cannot exist without forgiveness. A thriving family is pruned and blooms through it.

TELLING GOD "I'M SORRY"

> Now a man named Ananias, together with his wife Sapphira, also sold a piece of property. With his wife's knowledge he kept back part of the money for himself, but brought the rest and put it at the apostles' feet. Then Peter said, "Ananias, how is it Satan has so filled your heart that you have *lied to the Holy Spirit* and have kept for yourself some of the money you received for the land? Didn't it belong to you before it was sold? And after it was sold, wasn't the money at your disposal? What made you think of doing such a thing? *You have not lied just to human beings but to God.*" (Acts 5:1–4, NIV, emphasis added)

I remember the first time I read that last verse. I stared at the words and reread them. Sometimes I sought God's forgiveness, but other times I separated my behavior toward someone from having anything to do with God. That day my perspective changed: What I say and do is first toward God.

When we offend someone, we offend God. God loves us despite our sin, but our relationship needs restoration. As we approach him, we honor and love him. We humbly see our weakness and realize only he can change our heart. Only he can heal us. We demonstrate that our faith is in him, even if it is the faith of a mustard seed.

It did not take long to realize that a perspective change does not equal a behavior change. However, I was glad to be at a new beginning place. This prompted me to teach my children, so we could learn together.

I knew this training could become time consuming. The potential outcome outweighs the labor. When a child prays, God responds. He delights when a child learns to come to him and grows her seeds of faith. We might not know it; our child might not know it. As we teach our child to seek God's forgiveness, we connect her to the only One who can transform her heart.

Practice: Prayer Conversation to Say "I'm Sorry" to God:

Explanation to your child:

> *Mommy and Daddy teach you to obey us. Do you know who we are supposed to obey? God. In fact, God is the One we all have to obey. It is hard for us to obey God every day—just like it is hard for you to obey us sometimes, right? When Mommy or Daddy does something wrong, or we hurt someone's feelings, we tell God we are sorry and ask for his forgiveness. We ask the person to forgive us too. So, from now on, I am going to help you learn to tell God that you are sorry and ask for his forgiveness too.*

Example: A child talks back. First, discuss the behavior. She knows a consequence may follow the forgiveness conversation. If the circumstance is major, it is wise to postpone the forgiveness conversation until everyone involved is emotionally ready.

Mom: "You talked back to me. What do you need to do now?"

Child: "Tell God I'm sorry."

Mom: "That's right. Do you want me to help you with the words? You can say the words after me."

Child: "Dear Jesus, I'm sorry that I talked back to Mommy. Please forgive me."

Mom: "God forgives you. He has erased it from his mind."

Intentionally look at your child and *smile*. I love this moment. Even if our child seems to only say the prayer because we said to, God works in her heart through her willingness to pray.

This is an important principle to teach older children too. Jesus presents forgiveness as a command to obey in demonstration of our love for God. Introduce forgiveness to a child the same way. Explain that we are not our own boss; we are under God's authority just as the child is under ours and under God's. Share how every day we try to obey Jesus' command to forgive. This helps the child begin to understand that we have to obey too. Communicate expectation of effort by likening this to our effort to respect and obey Jesus' command.

Two issues can affect a child's willingness to pray with you. First, build intimacy. When our child trusts us, she is open to what we introduce. Second, pray aloud throughout the day when you are with your child so that prayer becomes familiar and ordinary, rather than reserved for specific occasions, like meals or bedtime. Encourage all effort: "I love to pray with you" or "Thank you for praying with me."

If the child is older when you introduce this type of prayer, he may be closed to praying with you. Encourage him to talk to God and pray fervently that he will. Supply relational examples to help him see the benefit of forgiveness and the effects of the absence of forgiveness. Use family examples, characters in movies or books, or personal experiences from his past. When a child seeks your forgiveness, after you forgive, gently add, "Remember to talk to God too. He helps me, and I know he will help you."

BROTHERLY LOVE

I used to joke with Terrell that the children are trying to get along to avoid having to apologize to each other. Our three children were together a lot as they grew up. Peace prevailed some days, and others were really hard. Hurt, conflict, and learning how to get along were components of their growing up together. Learning to practice forgiveness was too.

"Finally, all of you, have unity of mind, sympathy, brotherly love, a tender heart, and a humble mind" (1 Peter 3:8).

Whew, that is a tall order. The people who received this instruction were not siblings necessarily, but they loved God. Some of us might consider the phrase "brotherly love" an oxymoron if love is not the first or second word that comes to mind when we think of our brother or sister. Rest assured, ample examples throughout Scripture describe hard, hurtful sibling relationships. Each reflects how jealously, hurt, pride, misunderstanding, and unforgiveness wreak havoc within family. Your family does not have to be like this. Opportunity abounds to learn how to love as we live with our family. Our role is to facilitate this. Family is the first place our children experience relationship. We can help them experience brotherly love as God intends it. A significant way they give and experience love is through forgiveness.

SIBLING FORGIVENESS

The home is where our children see and experience every side of each other's character. They behave like they really feel. Their mood is evident. They seldom filter their thoughts and feelings before these become words and behavior. They unintentionally take one another for granted.

We want our home to be the children's safe place, where they can completely relax and be themselves. However, love and respect are essential, and this uniquely challenges siblings.

Siblings disagree or don't get along at times for many reasons: They spend more time with each other than they do with anyone else, so it stands to reason that the potential for conflict is higher. If they have an issue with anyone outside the home, they tend to vent their frustration on a family member—rather than speak with the friend, teacher, or coach with whom they have the issue. If they are stressed about something like a peer issue, a deadline, academics, or a decision, they often release that stress onto a family member.

Conflict, hurt, and misunderstanding occur in our homes for these and other reasons. Siblings face the *hard* work of negotiating their differences, issues, and wounds regarding each other. Through each circumstance God loves us as he shapes our wills, molds our hearts, and grows our relationships.

Here is a four-step conversation I taught our children. Persevere through the initial season in which they learn what to say to each other. Once they learn this, they know what is necessary and expected before they resume play or another activity.

Practice: Forgiveness Conversation

1. Maintain eye contact throughout the conversation.
2. Tone is humble: A child's participation in this conversation will be initiated by us, so his attitude may reflect this. We may need to talk with him and give him a few minutes to consider his tone. Pray for God to impress his heart. If his tone is not respectful, say, "Let's try that again," or "You can stand by me until you are ready to apologize." A calmly spoken, firm boundary usually affects a frustrated child's attitude because he is ready to get on with whatever he was doing before the incident.
3. Name the offense and ask forgiveness: "I'm sorry I hit you. Do you forgive me?" Asking this question is very hard. Pray for grace.
4. Give a full statement of forgiveness: "I forgive you." Making this statement is hard. Pray for grace. It is not unusual for the offended child to say, "She doesn't mean it." My response is, "She admitted what she did respectfully, and she is willing to say this to you in front of me and in front of God. This is a good place for us to start."

When our sons were two and three years old, they had to "say their sorrys" more times than I could count. Ellison, the two-year-old, could not pronounce "forgive." He tried to say, "Terrell, do you forgive me?" but said, "Teh-wul, do you 'give me?" Misinterpreting Ellison, Terrell would respond with frustration, "No, Eh'son, you *give me!*"

Ellison tried to "give" admission of his wrong, but his pronunciation confused Terrell. As young as they were, they understood that each was supposed to *give* something. The unintentional pronunciation of "forgive" only accentuated this. The boys needed something from each other. Terrell needed Ellison's admission and apology. Ellison needed to hear his brother release him. Their frustration was poignant—and adorable. After translation, their play started fresh, not fractured with resentment.

The heart of the verbal exchange is the willingness to communicate and make an effort to be humble. This conversation is hard for each child—just like it's hard for us with another adult.

THE WORTH

Is it worth it? Without a doubt. Yes, the countless conversations are draining. Strong sibling relationships require effort. When we take time to train our children to exercise forgiveness, we positively influence the future of their relationship. They learn to deal with their experiences as they happen. Otherwise, memories of hurt and frustration pile up.

Pray—for the children and yourself. It is easy to get discouraged and frustrated as we trudge through these steps repeatedly.

A child might seek forgiveness with true remorse. Savor such precious moments. Other times the child denies wrongdoing and refuses to apologize, even though his sibling is visibly offended. Or, he eventually complies, but the offended sibling doubts her brother's sincerity and questions why she should have to say words to give forgiveness. As we watch, we might wonder if our effort to promote this conversation matters. It matters to God.

We can measure tone and attitude; we cannot measure sincerity. When a child obeys and gives words of forgiveness with an inkling of humility, be encouraged. God sees the struggle in the child's thoughts and feelings. Each time we help a child apply God's command to forgive, God impresses the value and effect of his Word on the child's heart. We teach; God shapes the heart.

One day our boys exchanged words of forgiveness, but over the next couple of days verbal jabs and rude expressions demonstrated that they still harbored grudges. By the end of the week, my patience had worn thin.

Lord, help me! I have prayed and done all I can think of! Pretty quickly memories of grudges I had struggled to release landed on my conscience. How quickly I forget my weaknesses; how easily I see a child's. I began to ask God to heal their hearts and help them let go of their offense. God always responds. Keep praying.

The struggle to practice forgiveness begins in childhood, but it continues through our adult years. Think about it. Have you ever refused to seek forgiveness because you don't believe you did something wrong or because pride covers your heart? Or have you struggled to forgive when the person does not appear remorseful? It is helpful to remember this when a child struggles with the same themes.

Hold on to God—and hang in there! As our children practice acts of forgiveness, they experience being held accountable for their actions. They learn that they have a responsibility to seek reconciliation in their relationships, whether they have been offended or are the offender. As children have opportunities to be on both sides of forgiveness, they begin to experience that reconciliation is fair. Each person has to say something and give something, whether they feel it or not. They learn to honor God and respect their siblings.

WALK YOUR TALK

Our children watch us; they record and process our words and behavior. It is important to live what we teach. We confuse them when we teach one way and behave a different way. They are likely to become less receptive or even ignore standards we present. If you realize you are not walking your talk, be humble. Admit it to God. Ask for his help to change. Sometimes a humble conversation with the children is necessary too.

Our five-year-old son Ellison provided my first lesson to *walk my talk*.

When our children fought with each other, Terrell or I required that they have the "forgiveness conversation." They knew the routine and obeyed, though sometimes begrudgingly. One morning Terrell and I got in an argument, and it ended with me turning my back in a huff, and my husband marching out the door to work. Unfortunately, the children witnessed the entire thing. A little later as I drove Ellison to kindergarten, he asked pensively, "Mommy, can I ask you somethin'?" I said, "Sure." He responded, "How come you make Terrell and me say our sorrys but you and Daddy don't?"

My heart sank. Guilt and regret flooded in. *How confusing for such a little boy. If these are the words he's saying out loud to me, what else has he thought about what he witnessed?* Ellison was referring to this morning, but I knew today was not the first time my behavior contradicted my teaching. Today I had behaved like a child; only, no one called me back into the room to make up with my husband. Convicted of my hypocrisy, I cringed with embarrassment.

As we approached his school, I acknowledged, "You are right, Ellison. Mommy and Daddy didn't do that right. We teach you and Terrell and Cecilia to say your sorrys. Daddy and I should too. I'm so glad you said something to me. As soon as I get home, I'm going to call Daddy and talk to him so we can say our sorrys."

Terrell was equally remorseful. After a conversation of forgiveness for how we had treated each other, we discussed the influence of our example on three sets of very watchful eyes. We made a plan to follow up at supper with all three children since they all witnessed our early morning drama.

During supper we told them that we said our sorrys. We talked about how hard it is to obey God sometimes. They nodded knowingly which made us smile. Then I said, "Daddy and I told God how sorry we are for how we behaved with each other. We also told him we were sorry that we did that in front of you, because we are supposed to be teaching you how to forgive." I thanked Ellison for how he sweetly asked me about my behavior, and he beamed at being told that he helped us obey God.

Next, I think we shocked them. "We want to teach you what God says, but we did not set a good example to you. We are sorry. Will you forgive us?" Unfamiliar with being asked this question, they nodded their heads—with open mouths. I will never forget it.

What we did not expect was the way our little ones engaged. Their eyes were fixed and they tracked with our every word. They were loving and so glad that Mommy and Daddy had made up. Terrell and I were humble, and their admiration was evident. Their response was God's grace to us.

> Clothe yourselves, all of you, with humility toward one another, for "God opposes the proud but gives grace to the humble." Humble yourselves, therefore, under the mighty hand of God so that at the proper time he may exalt you. (1 Peter 5:5b–6)

Children witness and process many experiences silently. Terrell and I are grateful to God that on this day Ellison processed his thoughts out loud with me. We learned a powerful lesson.

Through the years, God builds a relationship of mutual respect between our child and us. Our role is to lead humbly and live what we teach. The child's role is to follow humbly and try to learn from our example. When each of us fails, God supplies grace.

THINK ABOUT IT

1. Have you ever thought of forgiveness as an expression of love? How does that inspire you?

2. Is it a new concept for you to seek God's forgiveness?

   a. When you ask God for forgiveness, are you more peaceful?

   b. How do you think your child could be impacted when he goes to God for forgiveness?

3. If your child learns that you try every day to obey God, how do you think this could impact her regarding her image of you and her own relationship with God?

4. The forgiveness conversation takes a few minutes. How could this impact peace in your home?

5. Have you ever asked someone, "Will you forgive me?"

   a. Why do you think this is hard?

   b. Why do you think it might be hard for a child?

6. Four suggested steps for forgiving were described: (1) eye contact; (2) tone; (3) saying, "I'm sorry that I _____. Do you forgive me?"; (4) response: "I forgive you."

   a. What might be the biggest hurdle you'll face trying to teach and train this?

13

Forgiveness Between Parent and Child

HELP THE CHILD LEARN TO INITIATE

A CHILD HAS A forgiveness conversation with a sibling because we initiate it. When the conversation needs to occur with us, we initiate this too. Use a gentle prompt like, "Do you have something to say to me?" Sometimes the setting isn't appropriate to have a conversation, so later on I might say, "I think you have something to say to me about what happened when your friends were here."

We are making a disciple; we teach and train. You can use the same conversation shared in the last chapter. After enough practice, the child learns to initiate. Be patient and pray for him.

The Final Response

"I forgive you" are important words.

When a child asks for your forgiveness, pray to reflect God's unwavering love. He listens and forgives completely. He doesn't judge, reject, yell, or treat us differently. He wants us to learn from our behavior, so we may experience a consequence. He knows who we can become as we follow him, so his forgiveness reminds us of his love and hope for us.

Forgiven, we are to forgive—completely and with no conditions attached.

A hug, smile, and a few tender words show the child that that we love him, we appreciate his hard-to-say words, and we release him from the offense. As the child hears these words and sees that we mean it, she experiences grace.

A child will not say it, but sometimes she wonders how we feel about her after she's done something wrong. The child can tell—like we can tell—when words aren't authentic. Sometimes I I've said, "I forgive you" to a child, yet my face or attitude reflected anger, disappointment, or judgment. Reconciliation does not occur, strain is added to the relationship, and we have opened the door for the child to believe lies about her self and our relationship. One painful way this manifests is when a child begins to avoid eye contact or avoid us.

Some days I wondered if there was any glimmer of remorse when a child apologized to me. The decision to release our child in these hard moments is an act of obedience to God and a decision to trust him that he is at work in the child's heart, our heart, and the relationship. Saying the words helps us truly release the child from the offense. We demonstrate to God and the child that we don't want to hold the offense—for the sake of the two relationships. How we forgive influences how she perceives God's forgiveness and how she forgives others, including us.

Dealing with our feelings is essential, but separate from this moment. We need to unload our pain frequently to God, so that the emotional effect of offenses does not pile up. Faithfully, he restores and heals us.

FORGIVEN, WE FORGIVE

In Matthew 18:23–35, Jesus tells a parable of a master who forgave his servant a debt. When the servant begged him for patience to repay, the master forgave the debt. Then that servant went to collect a debt owed to him, but when that person asked for patience, the servant refused him and put him in jail. The servant's master learned of this, reminded him of the forgiveness he had received, and put him in jail. Jesus then summarizes his parable: "So also my heavenly Father will do to everyone of you, if you do not forgive your brother from your heart" (Matthew 18:35).

To forgive "from your heart" means our heart is changed by the grace we receive from God. Knowing what we deserved when we sinned, we realize the gift we are given instead. The first master forgave his servant's debt and exercised patience regarding his behavior. The forgiven servant's heart was not changed by his master's grace. Instead, the forgiven servant holds an offense against his servant. Sometimes we are like the ungrateful servant with our child. His servant's plea for patience represents our child's hope, as he anticipates our response to his misbehavior—*Be patient with me and forgive me, again.* We are relieved that God forgives our debt of sin, but we hold our child's offense against him. Pray for grace to forgive each child's acts of disobedience daily. When we choose to forgive and practice patience, God grows fruit in us.

Also, forgiveness cancels indebtedness, but it does not mean that consequences are lifted. God sometimes allows consequences that naturally follow certain decisions, or he gives consequences as deterrents. For example, we can tell God we are sorry for speeding, but we might get a ticket. If a child has not turned in his homework, he may have to stay after school to complete it even if he apologized to the teacher. If one child hits another child, a consequence to the offender helps both children see that hitting will not be tolerated. Other times, we might extend grace and withhold a consequence to have a significant conversation instead. Prayer helps us with this discernment.

FAITH TO FORGIVE

"You know better!"

"How long is he going to keep lying to us?"

"What is it going to take for him to see how hurtful his words are?"

A child repeatedly disobeys, or the theme of disobedience lasts so long that we are at our wits end. We are confounded—out of consequences, talking points, and patience. We know he knows better. Why does he continue to repeat this? He even admits he is wrong and seems to mean it when he apologizes. Each time we are hopeful: *This time he really means it. I think this is the end of the problem.* And then it happens again.

Jesus knew his disciples would get frustrated about how often they would need to forgive. He provides two steps: rebuke (correct) and forgive. Then he presses them further to forgive without keeping count: "Pay attention to yourselves! If your brother sins, rebuke him, and if he repents, forgive him, and if he sins against you seven times in the day, and turns to you seven times, saying, 'I repent,' you must forgive him" (Luke 17:3–4).

As Jesus' words sink in, the apostles do not say, "You don't understand, Jesus. This particular relationship is hopeless." They trust Jesus, want to obey him, and recognize what they lack: "The apostles said to the Lord, 'Increase our faith!' And the Lord said, 'If you had faith like a grain of mustard seed, you could say to this mulberry tree, "Be uprooted and planted in the sea," and it would obey you'" (Luke 17:5–6). They ask for faith to believe that continuing to forgive will bear fruit. Jesus understands their struggle to have faith and encourages them. He tells them that even if their faith is small, he will respond to their effort to trust him and try.

Almost every time I whined or judged a child for how long a behavior pattern remained, it seems God kindly reminded me of *how long* it has taken me at various junctures to turn my heart in the right direction. Funny how short-term our memory can be about our themes of willfulness and stubbornness.

Peter asked Jesus, "'Lord, how often will my brother sin against me, and I forgive him? As many as seven times?' Jesus said to him, 'I do not say to you seven times, but seventy-seven times'" (Matthew 18:21–22). Jesus' answer patiently prepares us that forgiveness is not a formula. If Jesus told us the exact number of times we will have to forgive any person, we probably would not get out of the bed in the morning. Worth noting, Jesus spoke these words as he was heading to the cross to die for an *uncountable* number of sins—the sins of all humankind.

We know better than to judge, be harsh, or hold grudges. Yet, we repeat these offenses against the Lord and others, including our children, over and over again. How humbling—our struggle is the same as our children's struggle. *Living the way we know we should is hard.* We have had a lot of years to practice, and we still mess up. Our weakness can help us understand a child's weakness and realize our need for God's grace to change our heart to love our child *in* his disobedience—the way God has loved us all our life.

Don't be deterred by frequency or longevity of a theme of disobedience. When a child admits his error and seeks our forgiveness, he makes two decisions—to obey and to be humble. This is significant. He is submitting to our teaching—and ultimately to God. Each forgiveness conversation means that child, parent, and God are engaged. He tills each heart and develops our relationships. Fruit is growing.

SEEK THE CHILD'S FORGIVENESS

Yes, you read this correctly.

There are occasions to ask for our child's forgiveness. Will this displace the respect our child has for us? Quite the contrary. Humility in authority is a very compelling trait. Aren't we compelled by the Son of God's humility to leave heaven, live here, and then die for us? God exalts Jesus for his humility.

When we acknowledge to a child that we have treated her wrongly and then seek her forgiveness, we demonstrate love, value, and respect for her. We relinquish pride or the desire to be seen in her eyes as perfect or always right. She witnesses that we care about our relationship. We also set tone and direction for how we desire her to live when she realizes she has behaved inappropriately.

Jesus describes how earnestly we are to pursue reconciliation: "So if you are offering your gift at the altar and there remember that your brother has something against you, leave your gift there before the altar and go. First be reconciled to your brother, and then come and offer your gift" (Matthew 5:23–24).

This is so hard! The word "first" always gets me. Here is one of my earliest memories of seeking my children's forgiveness—yes, I got to practice with all three at once.

Before church one Sunday, none of our three young children would cooperate and get ready. Terrell was already at church. At first my tone was calm, but as time passed so did my patience. I lost it. I yelled and each child got his dose of my angry looks. To top it off, we arrived at church five minutes late—and we only lived five minutes away. All of us looked nice, but my heart was filthy with anger. Their hearts were wounded and shamed.

Did my children know better, yet they disobeyed me anyway? *Yes.*

Did I know *even* better, yet I disobeyed God anyway? *Yes.*

Ugh! It is hard when you realize you have done wrong. What's worse is when you know you are *doing* wrong, and you don't stop doing the wrong thing. I already knew it was wrong to yell with a mean face to get my point across—*especially at my children.* I seem to become so much like a child when my children push my buttons!

In the church parking lot, I opened my car door to get out, but then I closed it. That Bible verse in Matthew came to my mind, and I realized, sighing heavily, what a fake and a hypocrite I would be if I walked in the church right now. For a brief moment, I reasoned silently that no one in there would know about my horrible behavior. But I knew. And God knew.

Sitting in the car, as other latecomers walked by, I felt guilty, still angry, but convicted by God's Word. I did not feel like dealing with this issue right now—in prayer or with my children. Yet I knew that true peace would only come once I chose to be humble and to exercise forgiveness.

Still upset, I turned to the children in the back seat, who had not uttered a sound, and I said, "We can't go into church like this. I am going to pray to God first. Then each of you needs to pray." Intentionally, I prayed aloud, "Dear Jesus, I yelled at Terrell, Ellison, and Cecilia and I shouldn't have. I am still angry with them for not obeying me at home, but I give that to you. I am sorry. Please forgive me, and I choose to forgive them." I wanted them to hear and see that I still struggled with my feelings but that I knew God was the one to help me—that he was the one whose forgiveness I needed first. I also wanted them to hear me tell God that I forgave them, *before* they asked me to forgive them.

Then, one by one, I looked at each child and said, "Mommy was wrong to yell at you. I am very sorry. Will you forgive me?" As I spoke, I noticed genuine calm filled my heart. Only God could do this. Each child softly answered, "Yes." Next, one by one they prayed, admitted what they were sorry for, and asked God's forgiveness. With my cue, each of them asked me for forgiveness. We were late for the service, but we entered God's house reconciled to him and to one another. The peace in my heart and toward my children was amazing.

"Humble yourselves before the Lord and he will exalt you" (James 4:10). God helps us know when he wants us to have a conversation like this with a child. With humility we respond to him and go to our child.

He knows we want to maintain our position of authority and have the respect of our child. He wants this for us. However, he calls us to live in a manner that reflects the character of Jesus Christ. It is through this submission of humility that we receive the respect of our child and God's blessing on this relationship. If you wrestle with this concept in general, perhaps the following examples will help.

Practice: Reflect and Pray to Seek Forgiveness

- Example: If I apologize, he will think he won.

Reflect: As a family we learn to love and help one another. When we aim to win arguments, pride is our partner. Humility paves a path to respect because the hearer knows it is hard to be humble.

Pray: "Dear God, I see my pride and I repent of that. Help me be humble and open to being wrong."

- Example: She will not respect me.

  Reflect: If we hesitate to apologize, we might be insecure about our standing with a child. In other words, the absence of respect may already be an issue between us.

  Pray: "God, I already think she doesn't respect me very much, and I think this would only add to that. Now I realize that I really need your help to get our relationship to a healthier place. Teach me how to be parent with the authority that you have given me. Please grow in her heart a healthy respect for me."

- Example: I don't feel like apologizing; I am still mad. It will not do any good anyway. Besides there are so many things she has never apologized for.

  Reflect: It's important to remember we are the adult—many years older than our child. God helps us know when he wants us to seek a child's forgiveness. Our decision to obey shows love and submission to him.

  Pray: "Lord, I do not want to apologize to her, but I do want to obey you. I give you my feelings. Fill me with your grace to trust and follow your way. Help me see my child the way you do."

THINK ABOUT IT

1. What, if anything, do you see as the difference between telling someone that you're sorry and asking him to forgive you?

2. When you tell someone, "I forgive you," do you sense peace in your heart afterwards?

3. Have you ever withheld forgiveness, waiting to see evidence of remorse or repentance?

   a. If so, how did this benefit you or the relationship?

   b. As you waited, was your heart peaceful or distractedly focused on the person?

4. Have you ever had an experience with your child whereby you forgave him and could see a difference in your child (for example, in his facial expression, attitude, behavior)?

5. Have you ever thought of forgiveness as a demonstration of patience and hope? Journal about how you understand this.

14

Tending Our Heart

I USED TO CARRY a large pocketbook, which enabled me to carry anything I could possibly need. One day I started experiencing neck pain, and as days turned into weeks I went to a doctor. He pointed out that the weight of my purse contributed to my problem. I followed his advice and downsized my bag significantly. It sounds silly, I know, but it was hard to remove items that I was used to having with me all the time. His council proved correct. When I carried less weight, my neck pain subsided. Unloading the unnecessary brought relief.

Emotional baggage can be just as subtle. Painful, confusing, or unresolved experiences are recorded and accumulate in our heart. The embedded emotions that develop around these experiences reside there too. Often we do not realize that emotional baggage is weighing us down and impacting how we think, make decisions, and function. If we are aware of this burden, we may not be sure how to address it. We want to deal with it—and we don't.

The good news is we can unload our burden to God. He gently shows us what we need to release to him. He prompts us to forgive or seek forgiveness or both. Faithfully, he heals us and leads us to freedom. The release and forgiveness may be hard because our grudge, resentment, or identity as the victim is lodged deeply in our heart. Until we deal with our wounds and offenses, they remain part of us. They influence how we relate toward the person involved and perhaps towards others.

The condition of our heart influences how we live in relationship with each child.

Many of our experiences as moms are fun, satisfying, and rewarding. We hold these experiences like treasure. When disappointment, disagreement, or hurt color our day, it is wise to take these experiences and feelings to God. When we hold them, they become baggage. If we process our pain with God, each following conflict is a *new* experience to process. Otherwise, each following conflict is added to the growing pile of unresolved and suppressed experiences and emotions.

God knows the heart of humanity. He told the prophet Jeremiah, "The heart is deceitful above all things" (Jeremiah 17:9a). God knows we will trust people and have that trust broken. He knows we will offend and be offended many times. We will be insincere and experience insincerity. His command to practice forgiveness compels us to look beyond people, to look beyond ourself, and to trust him.

UNLOAD

A child does not set out to hurt or offend us. If our two-year-old does not take a nap, it is not a preconceived plan. Yet her behavior disappoints or even angers us because we are not getting our way. When a child disobeys repeatedly, she is not trying to hurt or discourage us. If a teenager's only words to us are complaints, this does not mean she woke up plotting to annoy us. Still, our feelings of hurt, discouragement, or even anger are real.

Our child's words and behavior affect us. We feel deeply because we love her so much. Some of us receive each comment or behavior personally and react immediately with strong emotion. Others suppress their hurt and justify the offense by noting the child's age or a circumstance that he is going through. Over time, despondency seeps in or complaints seep out due to pent-up hurt or dissatisfaction.

Unattended disappointment can lead to discouragement. Unresolved hurt often triggers anger. Unaddressed anger can harden our heart. God sees the struggle in our heart. He knows how our feelings can impact our perspective, words, and actions. He wants to help us.

We need to know we need God, so that we will go to him. The same is true for our child: She needs to know she needs us, so that she will come to us—and one day turn to God.

When we unload to God, we demonstrate that we believe he receives our burdens, restores our heart, and provides perspective to help us move forward. Some themes of struggle with a child can go on for a while. It is a good practice to offer prayers of release and forgiveness as frequently as needed. Here is a procedure I find helpful. Use your own words, but I have included an example.

Practice: Prayer for Release and Healing

1. Invite God to reveal all that you need to unload: "God, please show me everything that bothers me, hurts me, or makes me angry."

2. Describe to God what comes to mind. Say it out loud or write it down: "God, I am hurt by the way my daughter talks to me. It has been going on for so long. I am angry with her. I am disappointed in myself for how I am handling this. I am discouraged because I don't know what else to do."

3. Release your burden and feelings to God: "I give all of this to you."

4. Choose to forgive the child: "I choose to forgive her."

5. Pray for healing: "God, please heal me." Some healing takes awhile, just like some physical wounds take longer to heal than others. Continue to pray until you have peace.

6. Pray for the child: "God, thank you for my daughter. Please heal her where I have hurt and confused her. Change her heart and help her turn from her pattern. Please change my heart too, and help me stop my unhealthy patterns. Please grow our relationship strong."

FORGIVE THE CHILD

When our hurt, disappointment, resentment, or anger is unknown to the child, there will not be a forgiveness conversation with her. Our conversation is with God. He witnesses our experiences and knows what we feel. He also knows if we do not feel like forgiving our child.

He wants us to focus on him—not ourself, our child, or the circumstance. He is the way forward. To forgive demonstrates we desire to move forward—as an individual, with our child, and in our relationship with God.

"And whenever you stand praying, forgive, if you have anything against anyone, so that your Father also who is in heaven may forgive you your trespasses" (Mark 11:25). Jesus guides with strong words. He knows what happens in our heart when we hold anything against anyone. For our own good, he commands this.

"Do no judge, and you will not be judged. Do not condemn, and you will not be condemned. Forgive, and you will be forgiven" (Luke 6:37, NIV). When we focus on our experience, we empower our feelings—to judge, criticize, get even, or hold a grudge. Jesus knows how hard it is for us to entrust our experience and struggle to him. He knows our exact feelings toward our child. We forgive because we love God, because we are forgiven, and because he commands this. When we do the hard work of forgiveness, we place the child and the circumstance in God's mighty hands because our focus has turned to God.

DAILY DILIGENCE

"Be angry and do not sin; do not let the sun go down on your anger, and give no opportunity to the devil" (Ephesians 4:26–27). God knows we get angry. He provides a boundary: Deal with your anger before the day is over.

God protects us. He knows what we are capable of with unresolved anger. The likelihood that we will be tempted to say or do something to cause unnecessary damage and division increases. When we hold on to our anger, we give opportunity to the devil to build a wedge between our child and us. Even if a new circumstance stirs anger the following day, one day's anger is less potent than built-up anger.

A daily practice of release is wise. Try to mark a time at the beginning or end of each day to unload experiences and feelings to God. Forgive and invite his restoration and healing.

> Put on then, as God's chosen ones, holy and beloved, compassionate hearts, kindness, humility, meekness, and patience, bearing one another and, if one has a complaint against another, forgiving each other; as the Lord has forgiven you, so you also must forgive. (Colossians 3:12–13)

Think of this as getting spiritually dressed for the day. When you invited Jesus to live in your heart, his Holy Spirit comes and dwells in you. Think about that for a minute. His power is *in* you. He provides power for us to deny old tendencies of our heart. He strengthens us to choose to wear these beautiful attributes provided by God. When we depend on him, we are prepared for the day. Clothed in his power and grace, we live the day.

Lastly, it is wise to share challenging struggles pertaining to a child with our husband and maybe a trusted friend. Their listening ear and support can be encouraging. Often God will use them to provide insight and prayer. The more we pray, our trust and hope in God deepens. He grows our heart to discern his prompts to tend our heart—with him.

FORGIVE THOSE WHO OFFEND OUR CHILD

We hurt when our child hurts: she isn't invited to a party; other kids tease or bully him; a teacher or coach is unfair; another parent is inconsiderate toward her. We comfort and help our child, but often we neglect to deal with our feelings.

It is important to release our child's experience and our feelings to the Lord. Use the same prayer format described earlier and substitute the individual's name. Otherwise, we may be tempted to judge, become bitter, or hold a grudge toward the individual. Forgive. Pray for your child's healing. Trust the sovereignty of God and what he *allows* to be the experiences of our child's life. Pray to discern how to participate with God when your child walks through a challenging circumstance. God always is working his plan, and the best way we can help is to pray, wait, and follow his lead.

THINK ABOUT IT

1. Have you ever thought of sharing your feelings with God and then unloading them to him?

    a. Why do you think he wants us to take the time to do this?

    b. If your child were to share the painful feelings of her heart with you, how would you feel? What would you want to do for her?

    c. When God hears you, can you imagine his pleasure that you trust him to comfort you?

2. How can regularly unloading our disappointments and offenses to God contribute to our feeling more peaceful in challenging seasons?

3. Do you think there are some circumstances with your child that have actually hurt you—but without resolving them, your feelings turned to anger? If so, describe the hurt to God, forgive your child, and ask for God to heal you.

4. When you decide to forgive your child, do you sense the hope that you are choosing?

15

The Beauty of Redemption

"I WISH I KNEW all of this years ago when my daughters were little. Now they are teenagers and I can't do anything about the past."

We have regrets. Decisions we made. Words we never spoke— or wish we could take back. We would like a redo for the way we handled some things. We wish we knew then what we know now. Some events are recent and others old.

God is timeless. To him all of time *is*. He sees our entire life, not segments. When we invite him into a segment or memory of our life, however long ago, he knows that time. He was there; he is here with us in the present; he is in the future. He is with us always.

When we pray, God responds. He wants us to approach his throne of grace. We can talk to him about the past, present, and future. Regret is not the end of the story. Our past is not a missed opportunity for God's forgiveness and healing. His love, grace, and power are beyond our comprehension.

"In him we have redemption through his blood, the forgiveness of sins, in accordance with the riches of God's grace that he lavished on us" (Ephesians 1:7–8a, NIV).

We have a Redeemer. His name is Jesus Christ. Through him, we can seek God's forgiveness and healing for any day or season of our life.

Jesus wants us to talk to him about these thoughts and feelings. Haunting memories rob us of the peace and joy he brings. We seek forgiveness for our past in the same manner we pray for present circumstances. Jesus died for all our transgressions—past, present, and future.

Believing God has forgiven you, forgive yourself. Sometimes it is helpful to claim this out loud. "Lord, thank you for your forgiveness. I receive it. Because you have forgiven me, I forgive myself." Otherwise we tend to hold our guilty feelings. It is as though God's gift of forgiveness sits on the kitchen table wrapped, because we will not unwrap and receive his gift.

In Christ, our life can be redeemed, and our child can receive healing. "He himself bore our sins in his body on the tree, so that we might die to sin and live to righteousness. By his wounds you have been healed" (1 Peter 2:24). It is a waste of time to worry whether our child remembers negative experiences or how our inappropriate behavior has impacted him. Instead, we take those experiences and our sorrow to God, and he reaps change. Through Jesus, we experience forgiveness and redemption, and our child receives healing.

Some of us have specific memories and themes that weigh on our heart. Others may have a general season in a child's life that troubles our heart. A lot of life has happened up to now. We do not need to remember every detail and cover every matter. At the same time, try not to make sweeping generalizations like, "Lord, heal all my kids of everything I regret before today." Be still and trust that God will bring to your mind the matters that he wants you to talk with him about.

Humility opens the door to healing and freedom. What an amazing Heavenly Father we have! He gives us the opportunity to look to our past with gratitude and awe because he forgives and heals. Here is an example of prayer for forgiveness and healing.

Practice: Prayer for Forgiveness and Healing

1. Invite God to reveal when and how you have hurt or offended your child: "God, please show me the experiences that I need to bring to you."

2. Name these to God, including emotions he may reveal. If you see a pattern of behavior, repent of the pattern. This expresses a desire to turn around from the behavior. "Dear God, you are showing me how often I yell at her. I repent of yelling. Please help me learn to respond with a calmer voice."

3. Seek forgiveness: "God, I am so sorry. Please forgive me."

4. Ask God to heal that place in the child's heart and memories, to restore her, and to restore your relationship.

5. Thank God for forgiveness, redemption, and healing your child.

6. God has forgiven you, so forgive yourself: "I receive your forgiveness, and I forgive myself."

7. Pray for God's help: "God, change me and help me be the mom you know I can be."

FOCUS OF MY FAITH

Recently, I walked through a season in which I was disappointed by the lack of change in one of our children. Heartfelt regret and a desire to change were strongly evident. The child genuinely sought my forgiveness multiple times, and I continually forgave. Early one morning as I was lamenting this circumstance, I glanced up from my Bible and noticed an old index card with this verse: "And without faith it is impossible to please God, because anyone who comes to him must believe that he exists and that he rewards those who earnestly seek him" (Hebrews 11:6, NIV).

I read it a few more times and pondered its application for me that day. Three phrases inspired me, moved me to repentance, and completely changed my outlook regarding relationships that challenge me. Through the phrase "without faith," God helped me see that I had my eyes on my child and his behavior. My eyes need to be on *God*. Faith is actively believing who God is. If I want to please him, believing is essential. When he wants me to see evidence of change in my child, I will. Until then, I pray and try to keep a clean heart. I repented of my pattern and asked God to help me focus on him. *God, change me through this relationship.* Next, "believe that he exists" reminded me that God exists in my midst *and* in the midst of my child. God works to lead and transform my child just as much as he works in me. *Holy God, you love both of us. You are shaping both of us right now.* Lastly, "earnestly" grabbed my attention. I knew that I spent more time thinking, sighing, and complaining than I did praying about it. *Lord, I am humbled that I do not pray about this more. I need your help as much as my child does. Teach me to pray earnestly.*

Long seasons of recurring offense with a child can lead us to shift our focus from God to our child's behavior. When we pray, God helps us refocus to him.

OUR ROLE

God called us to be a mother. He holds the design plans. Season by season and year by year, we learn our role. We depend on God because our learning curve remains large.

Sometimes we draw conclusions about our relationship with a child. We experience how she presents herself to us or gage the emotions she presents. We cannot see her heart, which means we are as likely to be accurate as not. The same is true for our child. She experiences our choices, moods, words, and behavior. She can't see our heart either. We know we love her deeply. Is that her conclusion?

"For the LORD sees not as man sees: man looks on the outward appearance, but the LORD looks on the heart" (1 Samuel 16:7b).

Go to God. All through the years, take your pain, confusion, conclusions, fears, and desires concerning each relationship to him, the One who holds the plan. His plan includes growth for the child's heart, our heart, our relationship, *and* each of our relationships with God.

The relationship between a mother and her child is for a lifetime. Healthy relationships grow as we invite God to shape our hearts. Pray for protection and growth for your relationship with your child. *God, help me be who you want me to be in our relationship. Lead both of us toward the relationship that you desire for us at this time.*

Think back to your youth. We needed our parents, but we did not think we did. We needed their smile at just the right moment. We needed their presence when no one was around. We needed those boundaries to help protect us from more than a few foolish decisions! We needed their listening ear when we wanted an opinion or needed to vent—even if we did not take their advice. We needed their hugs, pats on the back, and words of encouragement, even if we didn't acknowledge them. We needed to hear "I love you" when we didn't like ourself—or feel liked by our peers.

If your parents loved you like this, be all the more appreciative for them. You may read this and think, "I did not experience any of that." God can heal this place in your heart. Give him your pain, forgive your parent, and invite God to fill these voids with his healing love. He will. Whatever our experience was, we have the opportunity to determine what our child's experience is going to be.

Our child needs us, but she is not necessarily going to say this. We need the Lord, but how often do we tell him? Yet he is always here for us. He never leaves us—even when we live like we don't need him. No matter the age of our child, it is never too late to build, restore, or rebuild the relationship—with God.

> The Lord is at hand; do not be anxious about anything, but in everything by prayer and supplication with thanksgiving let your requests be made known to God. And the peace of God, which surpasses all understanding, will guard your hearts and your minds in Christ Jesus. (Philippians 4:5b–7)

Be filled with the peace that God generously pours *into* you throughout the day. Live held. Live loved.

THINK ABOUT IT

1. If your child shares an old regret with you, would you want her to know that God can restore her heart? Do you believe this for yourself?

2. How could peace become a fruit of admitting to God our troubling memories of regret?

3. Do you think humility opens the door of our heart toward change?

4. Why do you think it's so important for us to receive God's forgiveness and healing?

Made in the USA
Coppell, TX
27 July 2020